Game On!

Pat Doyle with Michelle Harkness
Canadian Intramural and
Recreation Association of Ontario

Human Kinetics

Library of Congress Cataloging-in-Publication Data

Doyle, Pat, 1948-
  Game on! / Pat Doyle with Michelle Harkness.
    p. cm.
  ISBN 0-7360-3446-3
    1. Games. 2. Physical education and training. I. Harkness, Michelle, 1962- II. Title.

GV1201 .D69 2001
613.7--dc21

2001024985

ISBN: 0-7360-3446-3

Acquisitions Editor: Amy Pickering; **Developmental Editor:** Myles Schrag; **Assistant Editors:** Lee Alexander, Jennifer L. Davis, Amanda S. Ewing, J. Gordon Wilson; **Copyeditor:** Jacqueline Eaton Blakley; **Proofreader:** Coree Schutter; **Graphic Designer:** Robert Reuther; **Graphic Artist:** Dawn Sills; **Cover Designer:** Keith Blomberg; **Photographer (cover):** Tom Roberts; **Art Manager:** Craig Newsom; **Illustrator:** Tom Roberts; **Printer:** Versa Press

Printed in the United States of America   10 9 8 7 6 5 4 3 2 1

Human Kinetics
Web site: http://www.humankinetics.com

United States: Human Kinetics
P.O. Box 5076
Champaign, IL 61825-5076
800-747-4457
e-mail: humank@hkusa.com

Canada: Human Kinetics
475 Devonshire Road Unit 100
Windsor, ON N8Y 2L5
800-465-7301 (in Canada only)
e-mail: orders@hkcanada.com

Europe: Human Kinetics
Units C2/C3 Wira Business Park
West Park Ring Road
Leeds LS16 6EB, United Kingdom
+44 (0) 113 278 1708
e-mail: hk@hkeurope.com

Australia: Human Kinetics
57A Price Avenue
Lower Mitcham, South Australia 5062
08 8277 1555
e-mail: liahka@senet.com.au

New Zealand: Human Kinetics
P.O. Box 105-231, Auckland Central
09-523-3462
e-mail: hkp@ihug.co.nz

We would like to dedicate this book to CIRA Ontario for its continued support in our development of resources, workshops, and active living in youth. As well, a special thank you to educators across Canada for organizing and implementing programs and activities that put kids first.

This book belongs to:

MANUELA VIDELA

CONTENTS

Game Finder vi

Preface xii

PART I THE MORE, THE MERRIER 1

Chapter 1 Ice Breakers 3

Chapter 2 Paired Up 10

Chapter 3 Assembly Spirit 16

Chapter 4 Old Favorites, New Twist 20

Chapter 5 Mass Games With a Twist 29

PART II HAVE A BALL 39

Chapter 6 Getting Started 41

Chapter 7 Teamwork 51

Chapter 8 Halfcourt Fun 60

Chapter 9 Ball Games With a Twist 71

PART III ON THE PLAYGROUND 87

Chapter 10 Fabulous Four Square 89

Chapter 11 Heaps of Hopscotch 106

Chapter 12 Fancy Footwork 124

Chapter 13 Off the Wall 136

Chapter 14 Outdoor Games With a Twist 144

About the Authors 161

GAME FINDER

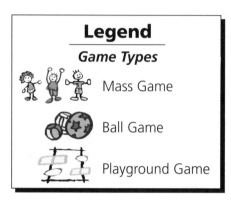

Legend
Game Types

Mass Game

Ball Game

Playground Game

GAME	GAME TYPE	SKILLS	AGE LEVEL	PAGE #
ABC		Agility	All ages	130
Agility Breakdown		Agility	All ages	11
All-Out Soccer		Footwork, running, strategy, team building	Grades 3 and up	84
All Together		Footwork, agility, team building	All ages	127
Alphabet Hopscotch		Agility	All ages	122
Alphabets		Team building, agility, problem solving	All ages	4
Are You Coming Out, Sir?		Agility	Grades 3 and up	137
Bench Ball		Catching, passing, team building, strategy	All ages	61
Blob Tag		Team building, strategy, agility	All ages	15

GAME	GAME TYPE	SKILLS	AGE LEVEL	PAGE #
Body Language		Walking, team building	All ages	13
Bounce Eye		Agility	All ages	159
Box Ball		Rolling, team building	All ages	42
Bring Back My Body		Team building, agility	All ages	17
Bucket Ball		Passing, catching, team building, strategy	All ages	63
Caribou Skipping		Footwork, agility	Grades 4 and up	132
Chaos		Team building, agility	All ages	30
Chinese Skipping		Footwork, agility	All ages	134
Corner Soccer		Dribbling (soccer), kicking, team building, strategy	All ages	72
Dice Roll		Math problem solving	Children who can read dice and count to 100	150
Donkey		Catching, throwing	Grades 4 and up	139
Dragon Hopscotch		Agility	Grades K-6	107
Dribble Tag		Dribbling (basketball), agility, strategy	Grades 4 and up	100
El Reloj		Footwork, agility, team building	Grades 3 and up	131
End Soccer		Kicking, passing, blocking	Grades 2 and up	74
English Hopscotch		Agility	All ages	109

continued ▶

◆ *continued*

GAME	GAME TYPE	SKILLS	AGE LEVEL	PAGE #
European Handball		Catching, passing, team building, strategy	Grades 4 and up	52
Family Circle		Team building	All ages	21
Finnish Hopscotch		Agility	All ages	111
Follow After		Depends on activities chosen	All ages	6
Four-Person Center Square		Catching, agility	Grades 3 and up	98
Four Square (Traditional)		Catching, agility, strategy	Grades 2 and up	90
Four Square Switch		Running, strategy	Grades 1 and up	92
Four Square Team Tag		Catching, passing, agility	Grades 4 and up	94
Four Team Pinball		Ball rolling, throwing, team building, strategy	Grades K–3	76
Gator Tag		Catching, passing, strategy	Grades 4 and up	44
Give Me a Hug		Team building	All ages	38
Hand Jive		Agility, team building	All ages	23
Happy Ball		Passing, catching	Grades K–3	50
Heaven and Earth		Agility	All ages	112
Hit Ball		Agility, running, strategy, team building, catching, passing	Grades 4 and up	54

GAME	GAME TYPE	SKILLS	AGE LEVEL	PAGE #
Hooksy Ball		Kicking, running, throwing, team building, strategy, catching	All ages	78
How Is Everyone Doing Today?		Team building	All ages	18
Jump the Shot		Agility	Grades 1 and up	125
King's Court		Throwing, dodging, catching	Grades 2 and up	65
Ladder		Agility	All ages	114
Lap Sit		Team building, problem solving, balance	All ages	34
Marble Shoot		Hand–eye coordination	Grades K–3	155
Mat Ball		Passing, catching	Grades 4 and up	67
Newcombe Ball		Throwing, passing, catching, team building	Grades 3 and up	80
Number Hopscotch		Agility	All ages	123
One Hundred		Catching, throwing	Grades 4 and up	141
Ooh, Ah!		Team building	All ages	19
Pass Ball		Passing, catching	All ages	46
Pass Ball Run		Passing, catching, running	All ages	48
Penny Four Square		Agility, ball bouncing	Grades 1–4	96

continued ▶

◆ *continued*

GAME	GAME TYPE	SKILLS	AGE LEVEL	PAGE #
Penny Hunt		Team building	All ages	32
Pickup Hopscotch		Agility	All ages	116
Pin Ball		Rolling, team building, strategy	All ages	69
Playground Calculation		Agility, math problem solving	All ages	118
Putting Marbles		Hand–eye coordination	All ages	156
Ring Game		Hand–eye coordination	All ages	157
Rockin' Robin		Agility	All ages	153
Rock, Paper, Scissors		Agility, team building	All ages	25
Schlockey		Agility	Grades 2 and up	147
Seven-Up		Throwing, catching, agility	Grades 3 and up	143
Shuffle Butt		Team building, agility	All ages	8
Sideline Soccer Chaos		Kicking, dribbling (soccer), running, strategy	Grades 3 and up	82
Socked		Running, strategy, problem solving	All ages	27
The Snake		Walking, problem solving	All ages	36
Speedball		Footwork, running, catching, passing, strategy, team building	Grades 5 and up	58
Swamp Hopscotch		Agility	All ages	120
Tetherball		Agility, footwork, strategy, hand–eye coordination	Grades 3 and up	151

GAME	GAME TYPE	SKILLS	AGE LEVEL	PAGE #
Two-Foot Shuffle		Agility	All ages	145
Two-Person Center Circle		Ball skills, agility, strategy	Grades 5 and up	104
Two Square (Traditional)		Catching, agility, strategy	Grades 3 and up	102
Ultimate Ball		Throwing, catching, running, team building, strategy	Grades 4 and up	56

PREFACE

"Kids Come First . . . *All* Kids"

These are vital words that I, a physical education teacher of 26 years, now constantly keep in mind. It's almost a motto for me now, but that wasn't always so. During my early years of teaching in the late 1970s and early 1980s, I was consumed with the concept often emphasized in team sports that winning was a priority. I was extremely uncomfortable in that environment. This was a real dilemma. What to do?

It was in the late 1980s that I attended my first CIRA Ontario (Canadian Intramural Recreation Association) conference and my new philosophy took root: "Kids come first . . . *all* kids." Teachers I met were having fun in their programs. Their games were inclusive, and participation was emphasized rather than winning or losing. I was introduced to creative adaptations of traditional games and to coed teams—but, most important, I was having fun again!

The transition in my own program was slow to develop. Building a customized intramural program to meet all children's needs takes time, as well as the complete support of staff and administration. With an open-door concept at lunch, anyone who showed up could play. If fifty children came, I needed a game for fifty children. Often I had to change the planned game, and create or adapt a game to fit the numbers. New activities were needed to accommodate more kids while maintaining skill development, maximum participation, and fun. It was kind of "learn as you go," but the direction was clear. Intramurals, special days, innovative teaching units, and a desire to create an active school for all the kids had begun.

This book draws from three CIRA Ontario resources that were written from my personal teaching experiences with specific needs in mind. These games are

- appropriate for all kids (though some require the more advanced skills of older children),
- user friendly, and
- easily adaptable for teachers and youth activity leaders of all levels of experience.

Most important, they're all fun, which is too often a forgotten goal in game planning.

My goal for this book is to make it easy for you to improve your physical education programming, from intramurals to traditional asphalt games. This easy-to-use book brings together 78 games in one package, and offers teachers and youth activity leaders a variety of healthy options to achieve specific goals for their students. My entire teaching career has been spent teaching kindergarten through sixth grade, but many of the games intended for a large number of participants in part I (we often call them mass games) and ball games in part II are used in middle schools and even high schools. When I do workshops with adults, they enjoy the games as much as my students do. Playground games in part III are developed from the games children have played at recess for many generations and are therefore geared to elementary students. Detailed instructions for playing each game are given, including variations and safety considerations.

You may find any game quickly and easily by consulting the handy game finder on pages vi-xi. The game finder highlights the skills that each game teaches and the recommended age level. You can see at a glance the skills and grade level for each game, enabling you to choose the activity best suited for your situation. This format makes incorporating these games easy, so building up your own physical education program won't take as long as mine did.

Games for large numbers of people became my initial target because they

- included the entire school body, from student to custodian;
- could be easily organized; and
- could be completed in a short time.

I felt it was important to quickly find a way to involve all staff and administration in an enjoyable activity. I also realized the importance of school spirit when trying to organize other programs in the school, like intramurals and outdoor recess games. This spirit was present in school-wide activities such as those found in part I of this book, as well as other special events we planned in conjunction with those activities. I have some fond memories of children and staff who have made these days an integral part of my yearly program. Shy little nine-year-old Alyssa arrived at school on Bad Hair Day with her ponytails held out to the side by a coat hanger, forcing her to go through doorways sideways. And mischievous Ryan, on Record Breaking Day, started to hula-hoop at 12:00 and didn't stop until his bus arrived at 3:45 (that's right—3 hours and 45 minutes), and the entire school wildly cheered him on. Then there was our vice principal Mrs. Mark, who dressed identically to an eight-year-old student with developmental disabilities, and pushed her around the school in the child's wheelchair during recesses on Twin Day.

Being the president of CIRA Ontario since 1996 and a member of its executive committee since 1993, I should have a quality intramural program at my own school. The many games found in part II of this book are tried and tested in my own program. With the introduction of the gator ball, my intramural program has become an enjoyable and rewarding experience for all involved. My good friend and mentor Doc Schlei once told me, "Intramurals are the backbone of any elementary school." How right he was. They usually happen during the lunch hour, are open to all, have an active and social component, and are lots of fun when done effectively. Intramurals can and should involve all grades in an elementary school whenever possible. I have found that these younger children have unbridled enthusiasm and, when placed in this program at an early age, have helped make my present intramural program both easier to organize and more adaptable because of their earlier experience.

The playground games of part III go back to 1990, when my principal, Keith Murray, brought a game to my attention that I later named Schlockey. We made three Schlockey "arenas" for our students to play outside at recess. Today, the game is played in playgrounds across Canada, and has been written about by the Canadian Press, talked about by the Canadian Broadcast Corporation, and commercially made and renamed by many sporting goods manufacturers. Schlockey was the first outdoor game that opened my eyes to the real value of using the child's free time more effectively, and the precursor to "Awesome Asphalt Activities"—the CIRA Ontario resource that was used to make part III of this book. My school has Schlockey games, basketball hoops, tetherballs, four squares, hopscotches, skipping areas, and various wall games scattered about the paved area. Our playground is a smorgasbord of activities and a fun place to be.

Take your whole student body, or just a single class, or a small group of children. Mix in some school spirit and innovative games. Sprinkle it all with enthusiasm, motivation, and fun. It adds up to a recipe for success in any environment, whether in the gym or on the playground.

Teachers and youth activity leaders will get triple value from this hands-on, user-friendly resource book: mass games, ball games, and playground games that will unite their recreational community. The pleasant result is that the kids who count on these leaders will come first . . . all kids.

THE MORE, THE MERRIER

Andy Raithby, a CIRA member and good friend, tells this story about a school spirit day he organized as a mass activity for the school. Mass activities are those designed for a large number of people to participate, regardless of age or athletic skill level. Students and staff were encouraged to wear their favorite team sweater to school to celebrate Favorite Team Day. The whole school was colored with the gear of an array of professional and amateur sports teams.

   As the morning recess bell rang and the students filed out for their morning break, they were all stopped short by a remarkable sight. With his electric floor cleaner decorated in all kinds of Toronto Maple Leaf hockey paraphernalia, and a Canadian flag waving proudly from the side, the head custodian sat in a chair with coasters on its legs. He drove down the main hallway with as much pride and purpose as a Zamboni driver at Maple Leaf Gardens. This is the school and community spirit we try to promote with our mass appeal games. Everyone gets involved.

In the 1980s and early 1990s, Canadian schools regularly partici-pated in Canada Fitness Week (CFW). This week in May was designed to promote physical activity throughout the communities across the country.

People ran relays between city schools; entire school boards went for walks around their neighborhoods on Sneaker Day; and individual schools would plan their own activities to celebrate this special week.

It was this week that became the foundation of my CIRA Ontario resource "Mass Appeal—Activities for Groups of 50 or More," and part I of *Game On!* Schools were encouraged to create a mass activity that involved everybody in the school at the same time. Each year I developed a new idea for my school, and before I knew it there were enough ideas that we had daily assemblies and a mass activity every day of CFW.

Over time, with the combined efforts of staff, administrators, and the community, the activities were refined to be run efficiently and quickly without disrupting each school day, while bringing a renewed feeling of pride and spirit to the school and community.

CHAPTER 1

Ice Breakers

Friendship is a special place.
I am glad we are there.

ALPHABETS

How about getting together in large groups and spelling words with your body? This game is sure to be a hit with all ages, especially those who are just learning to spell. Letters can be formed by one person or by multiple persons.

Level

All ages

Skills

Team building
Agility
Problem solving

Equipment

None

Description

Divide your students into groups and ask them to form various letters of the alphabet by lying down and forming the letters with their bodies. Be sure to share each group's letters with the other groups.

After they have formed several letters, ask the group to spell a short word.

Increase the size of the groups as you make the words longer.

Whole groups can represent one letter.

Then, in an outdoor field or open area, spell the phrase by forming the letters collectively. For example, Port Perry High School spelled "PPHS" across their football field.

Variations

- Have groups of students spell out the words to popular songs.
- Use difficult words, like Kalamazoo, Mississauga, Tennessee, or kaleidoscope.
- Try spelling theme words for special occasions, like Valentine's Day, Christmas, or the name of a camp or school.

- Prizes can be given for the group that forms letters fastest, the easiest-to-read letters, or the funniest shapes. Also, prizes can be awarded to spectators who correctly guess a sentence, word, or letter.

- Standing on a roof or ladder, take an aerial photograph of the letters.

 ## SUCCESS STORY

At one of my schools we had the entire school create the number 125 to celebrate Canada's 125th birthday. We then had the picture enlarged, framed, and given to the school at a year-end assembly. It hangs proudly in the hall today. At another school we had the entire school dress in the colors of the Olympic rings. We then formed the Olympic circles on the pavement, took an aerial photo, and had it published in the local paper.

FOLLOW AFTER

Here is an excellent way to warm up a large group, team, aerobics class, or gym class, and add a twist of fun while doing it.

Level

All ages

Skills

Variety of skills, depending on the exercises you choose

Equipment

None

Description

The teacher or activity leader begins in front of the group, with the group divided into four sections. The leader demonstrates an exercise (such as jumping jacks) while the four groups watch. The leader continues the exercise for 15 to 30 seconds, then switches to another exercise (for example, arm circles). As soon as the leader switches, the first group on the leader's right starts doing the jumping jacks. The other groups continue to watch. When the leader switches exercises again (let's say knee bends), the first group starts the arm circles and the second group begins the jumping jacks. This continues until the last group has begun the jumping jacks and the other three groups and the leader are all doing different exercises. Once everyone is doing an exercise the leader can continue adding exercises.

To finish the activity, the leader simply changes the exercise again, but instead of doing a new exercise the leader stops and watches the four groups do theirs. After the required time the leader says "switch" and all groups begin to do their next exercise, except the first group does not have one to do, so they stop too. Now the other three groups are still busy. The leader keeps calling "switch" until the last group finishes the last exercise.

Variations

- The leader may do as many exercises as she wishes. As the fourth group finishes their exercise it is discarded.
- Try a different number of groups.

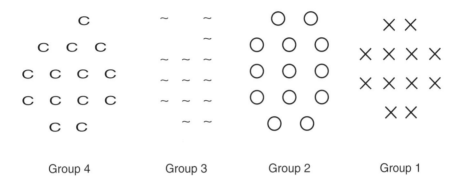

Group 4   Group 3   Group 2   Group 1

 Leader

► Keep the exercises simple in order that groups can switch from one to another easily.
► Avoid any partner exercises, as they will complicate the switches.

SHUFFLE BUTT

Shuffle Butt is lots of fun for any age and number of participants. The space required varies from a small room to a large field, depending on the number of people participating.

Level

All ages

Skills

Team building
Agility

Equipment

One chair for each participant

Description

Set up chairs in a tight circle (up to 20 maximum in one group). Each participant sits in a chair—except one, who stands in the middle. There is one empty chair.

The goal of the standing person is to sit down in the empty chair. The goal of everyone else is to not let the person in the middle sit down. The person to the left of the empty chair "shuffles" his butt into the next empty chair, as does the next person. Participants should be shuffling constantly into empty seats.

It ends up being like a domino effect of sliding butts, with one person running around trying to squeeze in. If the person in the middle is successful at sitting down, the person who did not shuffle quickly enough is now in the middle.

Start the game by having participants shuffle to the right. When the leader says "switch," shufflers must change direction.

At any point in the game the leader can yell out "shuffle butt"! When the participants hear this, they must find a new seat at least three chairs away. The person left without a chair goes to the middle. The game continues until time runs out or the group exhausts their energy.

Variation

Instead of yelling "shuffle butt!" the leader calls out a command, such as, "Everyone wearing green, move your butt!" Then all the people wearing green must find another chair to sit on.

▶ Do not use chairs that have arms.
▶ Be sure all chairs are snug to the ones next to them, and stop activity as necessary to readjust chairs.
▶ A proper shuffling method should be practiced by all before beginning.
▶ Hands should be kept between legs rather than on the outside of legs.

CHAPTER 2

Paired Up

Don't worry about people knowing you.
Just make yourself knowing.

AGILITY BREAKDOWN

This activity consists of several parts, so it is important for the participants to listen carefully to the instructions. The number of participants is unlimited as long as everyone has a partner.

Level

All ages

Skill

Agility

Equipment

None

Description

Form lines, with partners facing each other in opposite lines. The length or number of lines is determined by the space available and the number of participants.

Partners are identified as 1 and 2. Before the game begins, participants sit while the leader demonstrates how to perform the activities that will be used in the game:

- 1 around 2: Player 1 jogs around player 2.
- 1 over 2: Player 2 scrunches up in a ball shape and player 1 jumps over her.
- 1 under 2: Player 1 crawls through the legs of player 2.

The leader calls out an activity (such as "1 over 2"), and the partners perform the activity. Participants run in place while not performing an activity.

Leaders should vary the activities, as well as the order of partners (that is, call out "2 over 1" as well as "1 over 2").

When the group leader says "breakdown," participants assume the athletic stance: knees are bent, feet are shoulder-width apart, fists are clenched, and arms are bent upward. Participants should be absolutely silent and maintain a straight facial expression.

Throughout the exercise, the leader asks several questions, to which everyone must answer "Yes, sir!", or "Yes, ma'am!" or perform a designated exercise. Some sample questions include "Do you like to exercise?"; "Isn't this fun?"; "Am I the best teacher in the world?"; and "Do you all like turnips?" It is best to ask the questions while the participants are jogging on the spot.

Variation

For younger children, you can avoid the part about asking questions, but they love yelling "Yes, sir!", or "Yes, ma'am!"

BODY LANGUAGE

This double-circle partner activity is bound to elicit giggles and harmony among its participants.

Level

All ages

Skills

Walking
Team building

Equipment

Music

Description

Form two circles, one inside the other. Each participant is partnered with the person directly across from him, so that one partner is in the inside circle and the other is in the outside circle.

With the music playing in the background, players in the two circles travel in opposite directions—one going clockwise, the other counterclockwise. Participants move, or boogie, to the beat of the music.

When the music stops, the players in the outside circle freeze, and the group leader calls a body part combination, such as "nose and shoulder!" The person from the inside must find his partner and touch her nose. The frozen partner responds by touching her partner's shoulder. The last couple to finish the body combination must perform an exercise or other instructed activity before the game continues. Some possible exercises include jumping jacks, partner piggyback squats (in which one partner does short knee bends while the partner rides piggyback), or singing a nursery rhyme together.

Variations

- After several combinations have been announced, instruct the participants to find new partners and switch positions. If they were in the inner circle, they'll move to the outer circle, and vice versa.

- Suggested body combinations include:
    - Hand and ankle
    - Shoulder and calf
    - Elbow and back
    - Head and thigh
    - Finger and eyebrow
    - Wrist and knee

BLOB TAG

There will be no controlling this blob!

Level

All ages

Skills

Team building
Strategy
Agility

Equipment

None

Description

This mass tag game can be played indoors or out. Divide the participants into pairs. Instruct each pair to hold hands and form a circle. Designate one pair as the "blob."

Without letting go of hands, running, or falling, the blob attempts to tag another pair. When a pair is tagged, they then become part of the blob. The blob continues to expand until all pairs are caught.

If any pair falls, lets go of hands, or runs, they become part of the blob. If the blob breaks up, lets go of hands, or anyone falls down, they must stop until the circle is re-formed.

Variation

The game can also start with groups of three, four, five, or six people forming circles. This is especially handy when the number of participants is high.

SAFETY

▶ No running is allowed.
▶ If a free group falls down, breaks hand grip, or runs, then they must join the "it" blob.
▶ Tagging must be done by a slight body touch. Reaching out with a leg to touch another blob is not allowed.

CHAPTER 3

Assembly
Spirit

Do everything with enthusiasm . . .
It's contagious.

BRING BACK MY BODY

What better way to entertain a large group than with a song? This adaptation of *My Bonnie Lies Over the Ocean* is a great energizer to start your assembly.

Level

All ages

Skills

Team building
Agility

Equipment

None

Description

There are 20 words in the song which begin with the letter *b*. Have all the participants stand when you begin singing the song. On the first *b* word, all the participants crouch in a baseball catcher's stance. On the next *b* word, they stand up. They alternate standing and crouching on each *b* word throughout the song.

Teach the following song to everyone:

> My *b*ody just lies on the sofa, My *b*ody just watches TV
> My *b*ody is getting disgusting, Oh, *b*ring *b*ack my *b*ody to me
> Chorus:
> *B*ring *b*ack, *b*ring *b*ack, Oh *b*ring *b*ack my *b*ody to me, to me.
> *B*ring *b*ack, *b*ring *b*ack, Oh, *b*ring *b*ack my *b*ody to me.
> [Repeat]

Variations

- Add an arm movement.
- Innovate—for example, have students turn around or high-five each other.
- Sing the song faster.

17

HOW IS EVERYONE DOING TODAY?

This cheer will ignite an audience of any size and guarantee an enthusiastic response. It can be used at assemblies, morning announcements, campfires, or any gathering.

Level

All ages

Skill

Team building

Equipment

None

Description

Whenever the leader asks the question "How is everybody doing today?" the group always replies with this cheer. Teach the cheer in parts at the first full gathering of the school year, camp session, or whatever large group you are working with. The spontaneity of this cheer will create unexpected fun for a long time to come.

1. Raise your right fist and holler, "Fantastic!"
2. Raise your left fist and holler, "Terrific!"
3. Raise your right fist and holler, "Great!"
4. Raise left, then right, then left while hollering, "All-day-long!"
5. After the word *long*, take both arms and thrust your elbows back, hollering, "Ugh!"

 ## SUCCESS STORY

Our first-grade class was so accustomed to this cheer that on their visit to the fire station, the fire chief began by innocently asking how they were doing that day, and to his surprise and delight this was their reply.

18

OOH, AH!

This activity can be used just about anywhere with any number of participants, provided they've got strong voices and lots of enthusiasm. It's excellent for an assembly or gym cool-down activity.

Level

All ages

Skill

Team building

Equipment

A large utility ball with a good bounce to it

Description

Divide the group into two, and identify one side as "O" and the other as "A." Instruct the Os to practice shouting "Ooh!" and the As to shout "Ah." Challenge each side to be the louder and more enthusiastic group. Encourage proper oohs and ahs, not yelling.

The group leader then tosses a utility ball into the air. When the ball is going up in the air the first group shouts "ooh!" When the ball is dropping the second group says "ah!" At first the leader tosses the ball high and catches it, but eventually he allows it to drop to the floor and begin bouncing until it stops.

Variations

- Have participants add an arm wave movement on every turn.
- At Thanksgiving have the two groups say "Thanks" and "Giving."
- At Christmas they can say "Santa" and "Claus."
- At Easter they can say "Easter" and "Bunny."
- On holidays they can say "Holi" and "Day."
- Using a large beach ball will guarantee a slower ascent and descent.

CHAPTER 4

Old Favorites, New Twist

What we see depends on what we look for.

FAMILY CIRCLE

Based on the popular game Musical Chairs, Family Circle can entertain up to 80 players.

Level

All ages

Skill

Team building

Equipment

One chair for each family
Index cards (one per participant)
Music (optional)

Description

Set up chairs in a circle—one chair for every five participants. Leave ample space between chairs. Label each chair with a family name on the front and back. Be creative. You could base them on colors, animal names, or cartoon characters, for example.

Before the game, prepare index cards for each participant. On each card, write a family surname and a position in the family. Each family consists of five members: Father Smith, Mother Smith, Sister Smith, Brother Smith, and Baby Smith. For more fun, you can add the family dog and make six members.

At game time, randomly distribute family cards, one per player, and have players form two circles outside the labeled chairs. The circle closest to the chairs faces clockwise and the outside circle faces counterclockwise. When the circles are formed, play music to signal the start of the activity (you might want to try "We Are Family" by Sister Sledge). When the music begins, the circles move in opposite directions. If you don't have music, instruct the participants to "begin", or "go", and stop when they hear the whistle.

When the music stops, each participant must find his or her family chair and take a seat. There's only one catch: family members must be seated on each other's laps, with the father on the bottom, then mother, sister, brother, and finally the baby on the top (the dog sits on all fours with its head resting on the lap of baby). To continue, re-form the two circles and start the music again.

For more competition, play several rounds of Family Circle, and then begin to eliminate families: the last family to find their chair and sit in the proper order is eliminated. (Remember to remove the family chair when a family is eliminated.) Those no longer playing can help to judge or to reorganize chairs.

Variations

- Depending on the number of participants, you may make the families smaller—for example, father, mother, and baby.

- Have all participants hold their cards face down so they cannot be seen. As they walk their circle have them randomly switch cards with someone in the other circle. When the music stops, players turn their cards over to see which family they belong to.

 SUCCESS STORY

We did this activity with 80 eighth-grade children. Another teacher took the eliminated teams and began another game adjacent to ours. They didn't eliminate teams. So as our circle shrank, theirs grew.

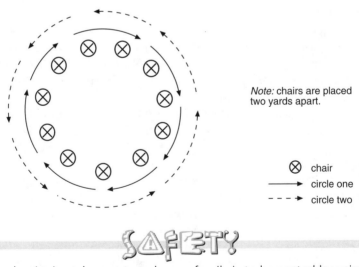

Note: chairs are placed two yards apart.

⊗ chair
⟶ circle one
- - - → circle two

SAFETY

Before beginning, demonstrate how a family is to be seated by using five volunteers. Explain that once a group gets its five members to their chair they may exchange cards so that a smaller person does not have to be father.

HAND JIVE

This hand activity can be done by an unlimited number of participants.

Level

All ages

Skills

Agility
Team building

Equipment

CD player and music: *The Hand Jive, Locomotion,* or *Old Time Rock and Roll*

Description

Teach each move individually, adding them to each other progressively as they are mastered.

> Clap your hands twice.
>
> Slap your thighs twice.
>
> Make a fist and hit the left fist on top of the right, twice.
>
> Hit the right fist on top of the left twice.
>
> Hold your hands out, fingers spread, and move the left hand over the right hand, twice.
>
> Repeat, this time putting the right hand over the left hand twice.
>
> Wave your right hand across and in front of your body.
>
> Wave your left hand across and in front of your body.
>
> Hitchhike with your right thumb twice.
>
> Hitchhike with your left thumb twice.
>
> Make a circle in the air with your right index finger above your ear.
>
> Make a circle in the air with your left index finger above your ear.

The finale:

> Catch an imaginary fly.
>
> Put it on your hand.
>
> Smack it.
>
> Lick or brush the fly off.

Start over immediately to the rhythm of the music.

Variations

- For added fun, do the Hand Jive twice as fast. Get progressively faster and faster to see who is the most coordinated "hand jiver."
- For younger children, reduce the number of moves.

 SUCCESS STORY

It has taken me several years to get really good at this, but I am proud to say that I am a really quick hand jiver now.

ROCK, PAPER, SCISSORS

Rock, Paper, Scissors has been around for a long time, but have you seen it played this way? The game is suited for an auditorium, gymnasium, or open field and can be played with any number of participants. There's no limit to the excitement!

Level
All ages

Skills
Agility
Team building

Equipment
None

Description
First, review the rules. A rock is a closed fist, paper is a flat hand, and scissors are the index and middle fingers in a cutting position. Paper covers rock, rock breaks scissors, and scissors cut paper. To determine a winner, opponents count to three and at the same time (on three) form rock, paper, or scissors.

In this variation, however, the participants play against the group leader. Instruct the players to stand at least an arm's length apart. The leader is in front of the group, in view of all participants.

To make a rock formation, crunch down into a ball. To make paper, stand up flat and straight. To make scissors, stand up and cross your arms and legs. Offer a few practice rounds before the game officially begins. The leader counts to three, and all participants jump up in the air and land in one of the positions (rock, paper, or scissors). Those participants who are beaten by the leader then join the leader at his end of the gym. All those eliminated stand behind the leader in scattered formation (see diagram). The leader places a hand behind his back and shows the group the choice he has made for the next jump.

The last player to be eliminated wins. Have different players take turns being the group leader.

Variation

Instead of Rock, Paper, Scissors, try Tiger, Elephant, Mouse. To form a tiger, extend hands as claws and growl. To form an elephant, swing arms together as a trunk. To form a mouse, hunch down in a small ball. Tiger eats mouse, mouse scares elephant, and elephant squashes tiger.

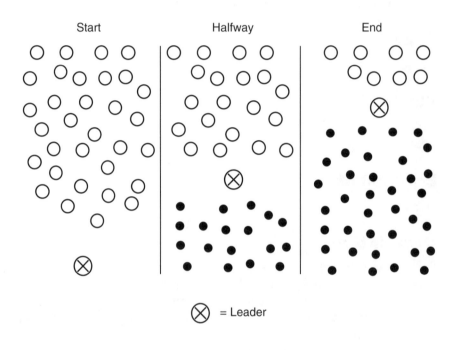

Start   Halfway   End

 = Leader

SAFETY

Lots of space is needed for this activity.

SOCKED

Capture the Flag is an old favorite that has many variations. Here's another that is guaranteed to keep everybody active!

Level

All ages

Skills

Running
Strategy
Problem solving

Equipment

Many rolled-up socks
Hula Hoops
Jump ropes

Description

To effectively play the game, you'll need a large open space and lots of old socks. The playing area is marked with two end zones and a center line. Each end zone is divided into two areas—one is squared off by jump ropes and filled with socks, and the other serves as a jail. The number of socks per team is determined by the total number of participants; one sock for every five players works well. If socks are not available, use beanbags or flags.

The object of the game is to capture the opponent's socks and take them across the center line to the opposite side and place them in your own roped area. If a player is touched by the opposing team while in the opponent's territory, the captured person is escorted to the opposing team's jail by the person who touched her. If a player has a sock in her possession when touched, the sock is returned.

Once in jail, a prisoner may escape only if a free teammate runs into the jail to retrieve him—they then may take a free walk back to their side. Prisoners cannot immediately run for the other team's socks upon release; they must first go to their own side.

Place several Hula Hoops on the field to act as safety zones (one hoop for every five players on a team). When in a safety zone, players cannot be touched. The player can stay in as long as she wishes, but only one person is allowed in each hoop at a time. A player may not step out of the safety zone and then back into the same hoop. The fewer hoops you use, the more challenging the game is.

The team with the most socks in its roped area at the end is declared the winner. Play continues for a predetermined time interval. A whistle terminates the game.

Variations

- Any long whistle blast frees all prisoners.
- Allow players with socks to use the hoops on their way back to their end.

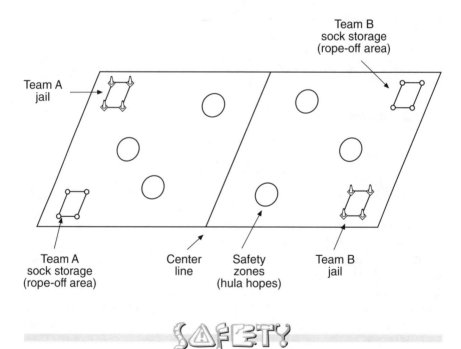

Team B
sock storage
(rope-off area)

Team A
jail

Team A
sock storage
(rope-off area)

Center
line

Safety
zones
(hula hopes)

Team B
jail

SAFETY

All tags must be made with two hands between the shoulders and the waist.

CHAPTER 5

Mass Games With a Twist

In whatever you do . . . have FUN.

CHAOS

If you want to create a little excitement and energy in a group, organize a game of Chaos! The game is ideally played with 50 or more participants in an open field or double-sized gym.

Level

All ages

Skills

Team building
Agility

Equipment

None (unless playing the variation, in which case you need refrigerator boxes)

Description

Divide the participants into four teams and send each team to a different corner of the field or gymnasium. Instruct each group to choose a team name. On the word go, each team tries to get to the opposite corner of the playing field as quickly as possible. The first team to get all of their members to the opposite corner is victorious. (The game gets its name from the chaos created in the middle of the playing area as the players charge to the opposite side of the field.)

When the group has successfully completed the first round, suggest using different modes of transportation. How about hopping on one foot, galloping, skipping, wheelbarrowing, or holding hands with a partner? Or add a different dimension to the game by providing varied instructions—for example, team A and team B switch places.

Variation

This variation is as fun to watch as it is to play!

Each of the four teams divides into pairs and then sends half of these pairs to the diagonal corner. For example, if a team has 12 members, 3 pairs go to the diagonal corner and 3 pairs stay. There will be pairs from two different corners in each corner. Each team has an empty fridge box (or stove box for younger and shorter children).

Place the box over the heads of the first two partners, who then must negotiate their way to the diagonal corner, where two of their teammates are waiting to bring it back.

The relay is over when all pairs are back where they started.

Note: the boxes can be folded and stored for future use.

▶ Do the following without a fridge or stove box so that all participants can see. First show how to position yourself and your partner (side by side) under the box, using your hands to support the box.

▶ Next, demonstrate how to rotate the box horizontally when you bump into an obstacle.

▶ Make sure no one runs in the fridge box relay!

PENNY HUNT

Want to make lunch-hour supervisors your friends for life? Organize a lunch-hour penny hunt—children are so busy hunting for pennies that they don't have time to misbehave! Penny hunts are one of the most popular large group activities, and are easily adapted to any setting.

Level

All ages

Skill

Team building

Equipment

- Several thousand pennies will be needed. You may get these at a bank; or, even better, have students collect them for their classes over a period of time. The collection can be used as a fund-raiser.
- Also necessary is a paper bag for each homeroom or class. The bags can be marked with the teacher's name, or any method you choose to identify teams.

Description

Scatter a large quantity of pennies in an outdoor grassy play area. Leave no space unturned, hiding the pennies both high and low. Sandboxes or sandy playground areas are excellent hiding spots.

During a lunch hour or other designated time period, participants may hunt individually, in pairs, by class, or girls versus boys. Each group has a bag to hold its findings. The hunt area can be sectioned off by grade or by classroom. When time is up, all groups return their counted pennies to a designated spot.

Prizes can be awarded as the organizers see fit, and the pennies can be given to a community charity or used as fund-raising profits. We sometimes get more pennies back than we started with, and children are often bringing us pennies for days after the event.

Variations

- Add another twist by hiding coins from other countries or silver dollars. Offer special prizes for the person or team finding the special coins.
- Try hunting for peanuts, marbles, seashells, or candy.
- Place all the pennies in a jar and offer a prize to the individual who can come the closest to guessing the total (one guess each).

SAFETY

Try to place the pennies where they will be found; you don't want them to be left around as litter.

LAP SIT

You can play this game with two participants, an entire class, or the whole school population. Lap sits are fun, challenging, and great team builders. We did this with our 400 students and it actually worked . . . for a few seconds. No matter, because the laughter and enjoyment satisfied our goal: to have the entire school try something together that was fun!

Level

All ages

Skills

Team building
Problem solving
Balance

Equipment

Some sturdy chairs

Description

If you plan on doing this activity with the entire student body, try a partner, small group, and class lap sit first.

For best results, have participants line up shortest to tallest in straight rows, with the tallest at the back. Students should be standing close together. On the designated signal, each student slowly crouches down until his bottom gently rests on the knees of the person behind him. He may place his hands on the shoulders of the person in front of him.

To assist the group, allow the tallest person to sit on a chair.

Variation

Have the teachers be the ones sitting on the chair.

SUCCESS STORY

When doing this with the entire school, we brought the classes out to the field one class at a time and formed a large circle. Each class had a chair for the tallest person. Once set up, we had all the students sit on the designated signal. The figure shows the results.

► Have all groups involved practice ahead of time.
► Using chairs will enhance safety.

THE SNAKE

The Snake (or Worm) is a great way to cool down a group of 50 or more. It is a slow and deliberate activity that encourages cooperation and communication.

Level

All ages

Skills

Walking
Problem solving

Equipment

None

Description

Participants form a large circle and hold hands. The leader, who is part of the circle, lets go of the hand of the person on her left.

The leader then begins to walk to her left on the inside of the circle, instructing others to follow when their part of the circle begins to move. The leader should stay within a yard of the circle to her left. All members of the circle will eventually be moving. This continues until the group has a coil look and the leader has run out of space in the

36

middle. At this point the leader tells everyone to stop. Everyone must continue to hold hands.

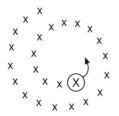 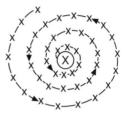

The leader then asks that certain members of the circle form a bridge with their hands so that she can exit the circle. She does this by pointing to the members who are in the path of her exit. The others follow her and the snake slowly begins to unwind. Everyone must continue to hold hands. All others follow as their turn to move comes along. The leader moves slowly and begins to form the original circle. As the leader reaches her original starting spot in the circle, the last of the snake will unwind and the original circle will re-form.

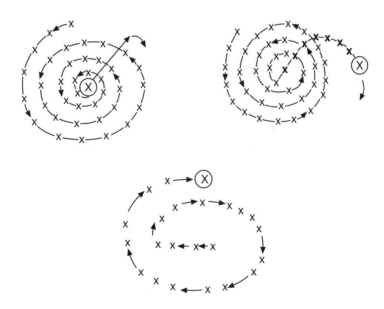

GIVE ME A HUG

Would you like an excellent and novel way to celebrate Valentine's Day at your school? Assemble the entire school population around the school, hold hands, lean forward, and give your school a *big* hug! This activity enables your group to use an entire school population in one unified activity.

Level

All ages

Skill

Team building

Equipment

None

Directions

Using teachers as leaders, have classes parade out of the school and begin forming a ring around the school. Be sure to include all staff, as well as any school volunteers.

When the entire school population has been assembled, use a common signal (such as a bell) for all members to hold hands; and on a second signal, everyone give a little hand squeeze and lean forward at the same time to simulate a hug.

If you do not have enough students to circle your school and hold hands, you could invite family and friends to join, or add jump ropes to complete the connection, or simply leave appropriate gaps in the circle.

For whichever idea you use, first have an assembly to outline and demonstrate **what** participants need to do.

PART

HAVE A BALL

My intramural program, offered Monday through Friday during lunch-time, drew over 6,000 participants last year. Each grade (first through sixth) had a designated day for intramurals. First and second grades rotated Fridays, and the other grades had their same day each week. This format enabled me to offer regular intramurals to every student in the school, and helped us achieve our National Award for Quality Daily Physical Education and CIRA's National Leadership Awards. Our senior students are the intramural leaders, and they run the program.

However, such a program created certain glitches that needed to be addressed before it could be successful. What would we do when 30 to 50 participants showed up at twelve o'clock, expecting to play? I needed easy-to-organize games that allowed for:

Large numbers to participate
Both elite and novice to succeed
Safety
Fun

This program set the stage for "Great Gator Games," a CIRA Ontario resource full of games that addressed these four needs. Although many of these games are played with various types of utility balls, I have found that the recently developed gator ball is ideal.

Many of these games are the staples of my intramural program (Hooksy Ball, End Soccer, Bench Ball, and Hit Ball). These comprise my games unit in physical education class, which begins every September. Other staff members also welcome these ideas to begin their school year. With a base of games in place, the intramural program is off and running by early October.

Whether they're called gator, superskin, crocodile, dino, elephant, or Eurofoam, these open cell structured balls are top quality, high bounce, easy to grip, durable, and stingless (I have seen children get hit in the face with them and smile afterward). These balls have helped make Dodge Ball games a safe, viable option in physical education classes. Many people have mixed feelings about playing any type of game that involves hitting others with a ball. Dodge Ball and Murder Ball are games that have been played for decades with varying emotions. I do play games in my program such as King's Court, Dodge Ball, and Ball Tag, but I only use the gator balls. Children of all ages seem to enjoy these games, and when taught in a safe environment the games can be enjoyable to all participants. Still, it is important to always stress to children the technique of hitting below the waist.

Many of these games are easily adapted to regular utility balls, and I have tried to mention this when listing the necessary equipment in these games. Keep in mind that with a harder ball the safety and fear factors become more important and need to be incorporated into your organization.

CHAPTER 6

Getting Started

With a kid and a ball you can do it all.

BOX BALL

Box Ball is an excellent warm-up activity, and it can be easily adapted to a full-scale game.

Level

All ages

Skills

Rolling
Team building

Equipment

Several empty cardboard boxes
Several gator balls or utility balls

Description

Divide the group into two teams and distribute 10 to 12 balls between them. Players roll the balls from behind their attack line (see diagram), attempting to knock the box past their opponents' attack

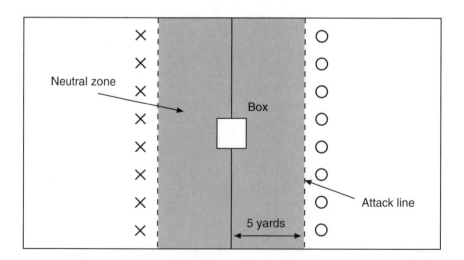

line. Players may go into the neutral zone to retrieve a stationary ball if the ball is on their side of center court, but they must return behind the attack line before rolling the ball. Players may not touch the box at any time.

Variations

- Use more than one cardboard box.
- Color code the boxes to allow for different point values.

Ensure that balls are rolled in an underhand motion.

GATOR TAG

Here's a game that encourages smart passing and strategic decisions. It takes its name from the gator balls that are well suited to this type of game.

Level

Fourth grade and up

Skills

Catching
Passing
Strategy

Equipment

Several medium gator balls
One bib marker, jersey, or "pinnie" for each participant

Description

The object of the game is to get all participants onto the tagging team. Two players, identified by bib markers, begin the game as taggers. They attempt to tag the other players with the ball, but they must be holding the ball when they tag someone (that is, they may not throw the ball at players). Bibs identify players who have been caught. Have the bibs handy in various spots around the perimeter of the play area.

Players may not run with the ball. Positioning and passing are important so the taggers are able to increase the size of the group that is "it".

When a player is tagged, she puts on a bib and joins the tagging team as an "it". The non-tagging players are not allowed to interfere with the ball in any way, such as blocking a pass. The game ends when all players have been tagged.

Variations

- To make the game simpler for the taggers, limit the area of play.
- When enough players have been tagged, add extra balls.

SUCCESS STORY

I first played this game with my fifth-grade students using two teams of three inside a four square game that was six yards square. The object was for one team to eliminate the other by tagging its players. This variation can be used as a warm-up, or it may take the better part of a physical education class.

▶ If a player falls down, he automatically becomes part of the "it" group.
▶ Encourage short, quick passes.

PASS BALL

Pass Ball is an excellent warm-up game. And, because you can change the numbers in the circle, it can easily become a full-class activity challenge.

Level

All ages

Skills

Passing
Catching

Equipment

One or more gator balls or utility balls

Description

Six to eight individuals form a close circle about arm's length apart. One person starts the game with the ball. That person passes the ball to another player, who then passes it to a different player, and so on. This continues until everyone has received a pass and the ball ends up back in the hands of the first person. Players may not pass to players next to them.

Now instruct the players to speed up the passing while calling out the receiving player's name.

Variations

- Add a second ball immediately after passing the first ball.
- Add a third ball or a fourth. How many can you successfully pass without dropping one?

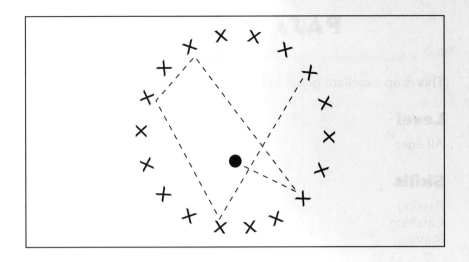

All passes should be with two hands and thrown underhand.

PASS BALL RUN

This is an excellent game to follow up on Pass Ball.

Level

All ages

Skills

Passing
Catching
Running

Equipment

Gator balls or utility balls

Description

Form a circle of six or eight participants about arm's length apart. The first player passes the ball to another player, and so on, until every player has touched the ball once and the last player has passed it back to the first person. Players shouldn't pass to the player next to them.

Once a pattern has been established (for example, with seven players, player 1 passes to player 4, player 4 passes to player 7, 7 to 3, 3 to 5, 5 to 2, 2 to 6, and 6 back to 1), the players are ready to begin the game.

Player 1 makes a pass and then attempts to run around the outside of the circle before player 6 gets the ball and passes it back to 1. So that everyone gets a turn, change the player in the 1 position frequently. This means you must establish a new passing sequence each time. Since a different person is starting with the ball, the pattern must be changed with each round of play.

Variations

- Have participants work on different passes, such as the bounce pass or chest pass.
- Have the runner dribble a ball around the circle. Start with the ball sitting beside the feet of the first player. When she completes

the circle, she can hold the ball over her head to show that she is done.

- Have the runner dribble to a basket, make a shot, and come back while the players pass the ball three times around the circle.
- Make up an activity the first person must do—for example, 10 jumping jacks; sing Row, Row, Row Your Boat two or three times; or pick up a rope and jump it five times.

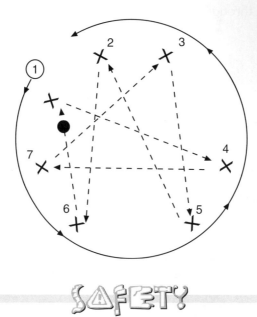

SAFETY

All passes should be made underhand and with two hands unless otherwise stated.

HAPPY BALL

Happy Ball is an excellent warm-up activity for teaching catching and passing skills to children in the early grades. It can also teach them to smile!

Level

Kindergarten through third grade

Skills

Passing
Catching

Equipment

Several gator balls
One hula hoop for each participant

Description

An unlimited number of participants may play, but restrict the playing area if the players are too far apart.

Each participant stands inside a hula hoop placed on the ground. To begin, give the balls to several randomly selected players. The players simply pass the balls around the gymnasium, but only to those who are smiling. Players may not move from their hoop or pass to the same player twice in a row. The goal is to keep the balls moving as quickly as possible without letting them drop. Use several balls to keep the game as interesting as possible. The game ends at the leader's discretion.

Variation

If a player drops a ball, she must jump in and out of her hoop with both feet five times before beginning again.

SAFETY

▶ Each player should call out the name of the player he is throwing to before delivering the ball.
▶ Pass all balls with a two-hand, underhand motion.

CHAPTER 7

Teamwork

Achieving teamwork and quality
is a marathon, not a sprint.

EUROPEAN HANDBALL

European Handball offers a more conventional approach to a team game.

Level

Fourth grade and up

Skills

Catching
Passing
Team building
Strategy

Equipment

Two floor hockey nets
Bib markers, jerseys, or "pinnies" to identify one team
One medium gator ball

Description

Divide the participants into two teams of six or seven players plus one goalie. One team wears bib markers. Assign one team to each side of the court (see diagram).

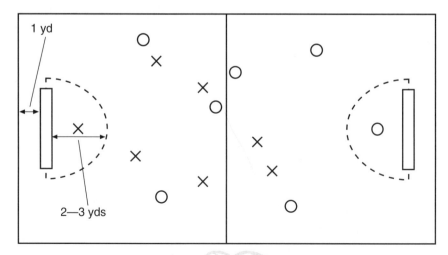

The object of the game is to score goals by bouncing the ball into the opposing team's net. Balls must *bounce* before entering the net. The nets are placed inside the basketball key, which acts as the goal crease. Only the goalie is allowed in the crease, and he may not leave it.

The game begins with a jump ball at center court. Players are allowed only three steps with the ball, then they must either shoot or pass. Players without the ball have total freedom to run. Defenders must stay at arm's length from opponents at all times.

If a pass is incomplete, it is declared a free ball and either team may pick it up.

After a goal the other team gets the ball and play resumes.

Variations

- Allow the area behind the net to be open for players on offense.
- When there are more than seven players on one team, allow substitutions.

▶ Utility balls may not be as safe to use in this game, as the goalies have little protection from poorly thrown balls. This is why the gator ball is recommended for this game.

▶ Players who fall down while carrying the ball lose possession.

▶ No contact is allowed.

HIT BALL

This is a great team-oriented game that works well as a lead-up game to basketball, as it uses the baskets and involves passing, space awareness, and team play.

Level

Fourth grade and up

Skills

Agility
Running
Strategy
Team building
Catching
Passing

Equipment

One medium gator ball
Bib markers, jerseys, or "pinnies"
Two utility balls
Two pieces of string

Description

Tape two defensive zones on the playing area, or use the basketball three-point line. At either end of the gym, tie up the hole in the basketball net and place a utility ball in the net. Start with a jump ball at center. When the game ball is thrown and strikes the suspended ball, a point is scored. The game is played like basketball without dribbling, but lots of passing, running, throwing, and shooting.

The offense cannot enter the other team's defensive zone, but the defense can enter their own defensive zone at any time.

The ball may be held no longer than three seconds, and players may take only three steps with the ball.

When a player is holding the ball, defenders may not touch the ball or the player. Encourage players to defend by keeping their body between the basket and their opponent.

Any infraction of the rules results in a change in possession.

Everything in the gym is in play, including the ceilings, walls, floors, and backboards.

Variations

- Players cannot score twice in a row.
- If the ball goes into the basket, and sits on top of the stationary ball without bouncing out it's worth two points (The leader should keep a stick handy to poke the game ball back out).

 SUCCESS STORY

I first learned this game at a physical education specialists course some 15 years ago, and it remains one of my favorites to this day. The kids beg me all the time to play it.

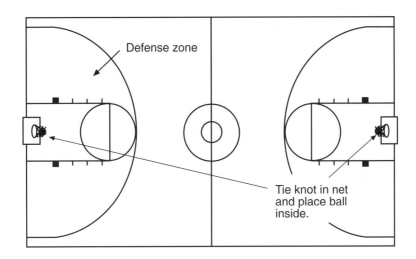

Defense zone

Tie knot in net and place ball inside.

▶ No contact is allowed.
▶ Players who fall down while carrying the ball lose possession.

ULTIMATE BALL

This fast-paced, team-oriented game is an adaptation of Ultimate Frisbee and is played indoors. In this game, as in Hit Ball, strategy and team play are important.

Level

Fourth grade and up

Skills

Throwing
Catching
Running
Team building
Strategy

Equipment

Bib markers, jerseys, or "pinnies" for one team.
One medium gator ball (A utility ball can be used, but players must have some catching skills.)

Description

Teams should consist of six or seven players. Extra players can be rotated into the game.

Start with a jump ball at center. Players move the ball by passing it to teammates. Opponents try to intercept or knock down passes to obtain possession.

The object of the game is to move the ball across the opponent's baseline. The ball must be passed into the end zone. It cannot be run in. Players must allow the opponent enough room to fully extend her arm when throwing. The ball is turned over to the opponents if

- the ball is intercepted,
- a pass is knocked down,
- a player takes more than five seconds to pass the ball, or
- a player falls with the ball.

56

After a team scores they hand the ball to the nearest player on the opposing team to begin play.

Catches may be made off side walls, but not the end walls.

No physical contact is allowed. Players should be encouraged to move their feet to stay between their opponent and the goal.

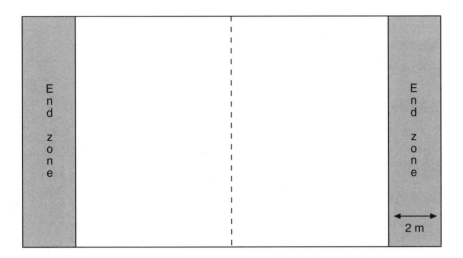

▶ No contact is allowed.

▶ Players who fall down while carrying the ball lose possession.

SPEEDBALL

Speedball requires that participants have some skill in both basketball and soccer. Once taught and mastered, it is one of our most exciting ball games.

Level

Fifth grade and up

Skills

Footwork
Running
Catching
Passing
Strategy
Team building

Equipment

Several gator balls or soccer balls
Two goals
Two baskets
Bib markers, jerseys, or "pinnies" for one team.

Description

Divide your group into two teams. You may have as many on a team as you wish. Each team has a basket, a three-second basketball line, and a soccer goal under the basket. The soccer goal can be a bench, hockey net, or a taped wall.

Begin the game with a jump ball at center court. The game is played like basketball without dribbling as long as the ball does not touch the ground. Players can advance the ball only by passing. When the ball hits the ground, the game automatically switches to soccer. In order to switch from soccer to basketball, a player must catch a kicked ball.

When playing basketball the players can go anywhere on the court, but when the game is soccer the offense cannot cross the defense's three-point line. A goalie can be used when playing soccer. Since players are trying to catch kicked balls while playing soccer, you may allow the use of hands in soccer. A soccer goalie may pick up a kicked shot and pass it to a teammate to begin basketball again.

Each basket or goal scores one point.

Variation

Make the three-point line out of bounds to the offense in both soccer and basketball.

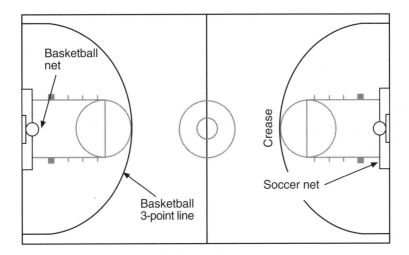

This is a no-contact game, and players should be instructed to follow those guidelines.

CHAPTER 8

Halfcourt Fun

Well done is better than well said.

BENCH BALL

These halfcourt games all feature two teams facing each other on opposite sides of a center-court line. The games require various methods of teamwork for participants to penetrate the opponent's territory. Bench Ball is an exciting, fast-paced game that will involve all participants and encourage team play. This is one of our more popular intramural games that allows for large numbers of participants and has many variations.

Level

All ages

Skills

Catching
Passing
Team building
Strategy

Equipment

- Several medium gator balls (older children may use utility balls as they become better catchers)
- Several sturdy benches: enough bench space to accommodate all of the participants. It's better to have some extra bench space available.

Description

Set up the benches at a distance from the center line in keeping with participants' throwing ability. Divide the group into two teams and have each team designate a catcher. The catcher crosses over to the opposite side of the court and stands on a bench in the other team's zone. A neutral zone surrounds each team's bench to prevent players from getting too close to the benches.

The object of the game is to throw the ball to the team catcher—if the ball is caught, the thrower joins the catcher on the bench and helps catch the balls thrown by their teammates. If a player falls from the bench, she must return to her team's side and try again. The game continues until an entire team is standing on their bench.

Opponents may block throws and intercept passes, but may not touch anyone standing on the bench or enter the neutral zone except to retrieve a ball. Catchers drop the caught balls into the neutral zone.

Variations

- Start all players but one on the bench, and have the one player on the opposite side with several balls. As players on the bench catch balls, in a balanced position, they join their teammate on the other side of the floor. The first team to get all players off the bench and back to their side is the winner.

- Allow players in both games to let a teammate go in their place. This enables players to help the weaker throwers and catchers. We call it "helping our teammates."

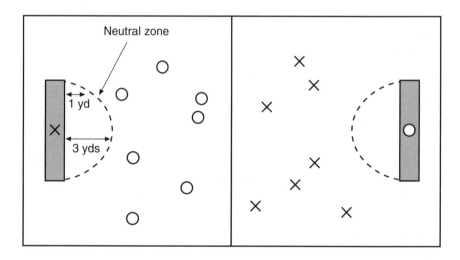

► Ensure that the benches are sturdy and that both teams can comfortably fit everyone on the benches before beginning the game.

► Encourage all players to use the lob pass from close to the center line.

BUCKET BALL

Here is a novel way to put those plastic garbage pails to good use.

Level

All ages

Skills

Passing
Catching
Team building
Strategy

Equipment

Two chairs, two Hula Hoops, or two small gym mats
Several medium gator balls or utility balls
Two plastic garbage pails with handles, or two large buckets with handles
Pylons

Description

Divide the participants into two teams. For each team, choose one or two teammates to stand on a chair, on a gym mat, or in a hoop and hold a garbage can or bucket, which serves as the goal. Use pylons to mark a defensive zone around the chair, about two yards in diameter outside the hoop. Bucket Ball is best played in a gym where the balls are contained by walls.

Players throw the balls from anywhere on their own side of center court (see diagram), attempting to have their catcher catch the ball in the pail to score a point. After catching a ball the catcher removes it from the bucket and drops it into the defensive zone.

The catcher may assist in scoring by moving the bucket toward the ball. Any ball outside the defensive zone is a free ball, but only defensive players may enter the zone to retrieve balls. The defense is penalized one point if defenders enter the defensive zone to block shots. One point is deducted if the catcher steps out of the hoop or comes down off the chair.

Change catchers frequently.

Variations

- Use several bucket holders for each team and scatter them in the defensive zone.
- Have each bucket be worth different point values.

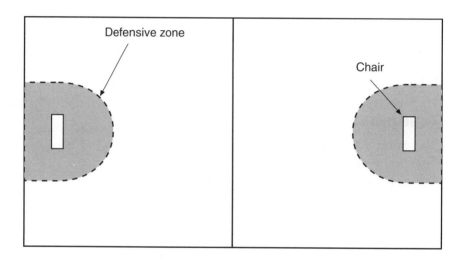

► Encourage lob throws.
► If the holder is standing on a chair, ensure the chair is sturdy.

KING'S COURT

This variation of Dodge Ball is fun to play because of the softness of the gator balls.

Level

Second grade and up

Skills

Throwing
Dodging
Catching

Equipment

Several gator balls

Description

Divide the gym in half and establish a two-yard neutral zone at each end of the gymnasium. This zone will serve as a jail. Each team begins on their side of the court. The number of balls used will depend on the number of players in the game; one ball for every eight participants is a good ratio.

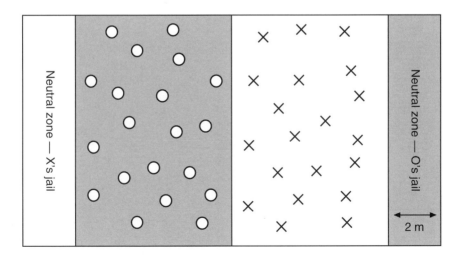

Players attempt to strike opponents below the waist with a ball. Use direct hits only—rolled and ricocheted balls are not allowed. When hit, the player immediately runs to jail behind the opposing team in the neutral zone. From jail, players can pick up loose balls or catch balls thrown by their teammates and hit opponents from behind them. The game ends when one team has no one left on its side of the floor.

Variations

- When a player in jail gets a ball and hits an opponent, she may run back and join her teammates.
- When a player in jail gets a ball, he may run back to his team with the ball.
- If a player catches a ball thrown at her, the thrower goes to jail.

All players must throw below the waist.

MAT BALL

This is a great game to teach passing, catching, and accuracy.

Level

Fourth grade and up

Skills

Passing
Catching

Equipment

Several 4' by 4' gymnastic mats
Four bib markers
Several medium gator balls or utility balls

Description

Place the mats at a distance from the center line in keeping with the ability of your throwers. The older the participants, the farther back you place the mats.

Divide the group into two teams. Two players from each team wear bibs and stand on the mats behind the opposing team. Create a neutral zone approximately two yards in diameter around the mats.

Each team remains in its court (see diagram). Players retrieve balls from the floor on their side of the court and try to throw them to their teammates (mat keepers) standing on the mats on the opposite side of the gym. Standing near center when throwing is encouraged since it makes for a shorter pass. Other players may stand by the neutral zone and attempt to bat down low throws. The mat keepers are not allowed to leave their mats. A point is scored every time a mat keeper catches the ball without it touching the ground. The mat keeper drops the ball into the neutral zone after catching it. The mat keeper keeps his own score.

Change the mat keepers frequently.

Variation

Once the mat keeper catches a ball, she returns to her side of the floor with the ball and another player takes her place. The first team to have all their players catch a ball is the winner.

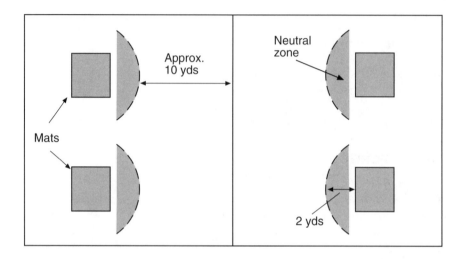

Encourage lob passes.

PIN BALL

Children love to block balls, especially with the soft gator balls. This game enables everyone to be a goalie.

Level

All ages

Skills

Rolling
Team building
Strategy

Equipment

Several wooden pins
Several medium or large gator balls

Description

Divide the gymnasium into two playing areas and assign one team to each area. Establish an end zone at each end of the gym and place three pins in the end zone.

Direct the participants to roll the balls at the opposing players (below the waist). When hit with the ball, players must sit down. Players who are sitting may block balls from that position.

When a team knocks down a pin in the end zone, sitting players on the team are rescued and can return to the game. The pin remains down. After all three pins are knocked down, players can no longer be rescued—a player hit with a rolled ball must stand against a side wall until the game ends.

Players are not allowed to guard the pins, but they may enter the zone to gather a ball that is resting there.

Variations

- Add more balls.
- Add more pins.

- Allow pins to be reset, but give points for pins knocked down and players hit.

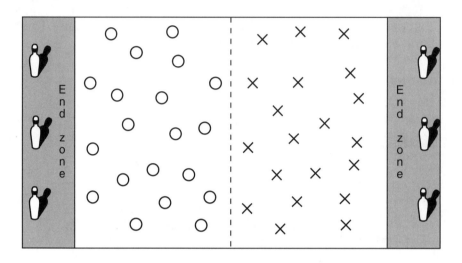

All balls must be rolled.

CHAPTER 9

Ball Games With a Twist

Everyone has something to offer.
You can't always be wrong.
Even a clock that stops is right twice a day.

CORNER SOCCER

These ball games and soccer variations offer lots of action and involvement, no matter how many participants you have ready to play. Corner Soccer is an excellent game for 25 to 50 players to review soccer skills and space awareness. It's one of our most popular intramural games.

Level

All ages

Skills

Dribbling (soccer)
Kicking
Team building
Strategy

Equipment

Bib markers, jerseys, or "pinnies" to identify four teams
Four benches
Several large gator balls (the softer gator balls should be used in this game)

Description

Divide participants into four equal teams and assign each team a number. Send each team to a different corner of the gymnasium and instruct them to appoint a goalie (or two or three). Turn benches on their sides so that the sitting part faces the playing floor. Neutral zones are marked with colored floor tape at each goal to keep the players out of the goalie zone (see diagram).

   The object of the game is to score as many goals as possible against the other three teams. To score a goal, players must kick the ball and hit the bench in the opposing team's corner with the ball. The game is continuous.

   Players can score on any of the other three goals. Players should move the ball by dribbling and passing it soccer style.

Scorekeepers stand behind each bench and count the goals scored against each team. The team allowing the fewest goals is the winner. (In our physical education classes, we don't even keep score. In intramurals, we have student leaders from other grades keep score.)

Switch goalies every three or four minutes.

Start with three gator balls and add more balls as the game progresses.

Variation

On one whistle, teams rotate one goal to the left while play continues. On two whistles, teams rotate to the right. On three whistles, teams rotate diagonally.

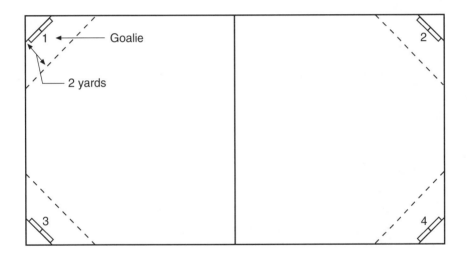

▶ Encourage low shots, as only those shots that hit the bench will count.
▶ Allow players to use hands to knock down errant kicks.

END SOCCER

This is one of the first games we teach to our students, so that they may play it in intramurals. End Soccer encourages equal participation and allows for large numbers and constant action.

Level

Second grade and up

Skills

Kicking
Passing
Blocking

Equipment

Several large gator balls (regular soccer balls or utility balls may be used, but only with more skilled participants)
Bib markers, jerseys, or "pinnies" to identify one team

Description

Divide the group in half and send each group to one end of the gym behind the goal line. Designate an "on" and "off" end for each team. Send three players onto the court from the "on" line to begin the game. The remainder of the players are the goalies. The goal is the entire wall. The height of the goal (waist high) is determined by the instructor. The "on" players try to kick the balls behind the line of goalies on the other team by kicking, dribbling, passing, and shooting soccer style. The result is three-on-three soccer with multiple balls and multiple goalies in an elongated goal.

On the whistle, the three "on" players immediately go to the "off" end of the line to become goalies, and three new players come on from the "on" line. The goalies continue to shuffle along the line, stopping shots and waiting for their next "on" turn. Goalies stay behind the goal line and "on" players must stay in front of the goal line. Goalies may use their hands at any time but should be encouraged to do so only to roll balls back into play.

Variations

- Add more balls (two balls for three players, three balls for four players, and so on).
- Increase the number of "on" players.

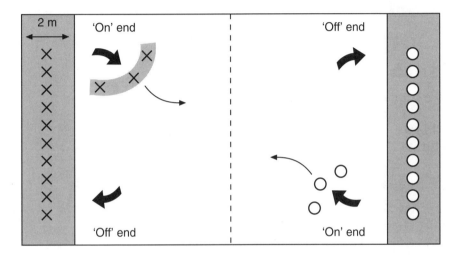

► Teach goalies to keep hands up and in front of them at all times.
► Players should be encouraged not to slide, dive, or jump to go after the ball.

FOUR TEAM PINBALL

This game allows everyone to play at once.

Level

Kindergarten to grade 3

Skills

Ball rolling
Throwing
Team building
Strategy

Equipment

Bib markers, jerseys, or "pinnies" for four teams
Set of pins (the more the better)
Several medium gator balls or utility balls

Description

Divide participants into four teams, identifying them as A, B, C, and
D. Designate team A as the protectors, teams B and C as rollers or
throwers, and team D as retrievers.

Line up as many pins as possible across the center line (see
diagram). The object of the game for team A is to keep the pins from
being knocked down. Teams B and C begin by trying to knock down
as many pins as possible in a given time limit. Team A tries to protect
the pins in any manner possible. Team D retrieves the balls. Throwers
may enter the playing field to retrieve a ball, but they must return to
the throwing area before rolling it again

Rotate teams, ensuring that each team takes a turn as A, B, C, and
D.

Allow the same time limit for each game.

If a player knocks down his own pin, it must stay down.

Variation

Reduce or increase the number of pins or balls.

| B B B B B | Throwers | B B B B B |

Retrievers

D A
D A A A
D Pins A
D 🦷🦷🦷🦷🦷🦷🦷🦷🦷🦷🦷🦷🦷🦷🦷🦷🦷🦷🦷 D
D ↰ A A A D
D A A D
Protectors

Retrievers

| C C C C C | Throwers | C C C C C |

SAFETY

The game is safer if you allow players to roll balls only, not to throw them.

HOOKSY BALL

Bill Hooks was one of the most respected physical education teachers in Waterloo County. Unfortunately, Bill passed away from a sudden illness; his students and colleagues miss him dearly. This game was one of his creations.

Level

All ages

Skills

Kicking
Running
Throwing
Team building
Strategy
Catching

Equipment

Sixteen 4' by 4' mats, 4 apiece for each of four bases
One medium gator or utility ball
Enough bib markers, jerseys, or "pinnies" for one team

Description

Connect four mats so that they form a base eight feet square, for a total of four bases (see diagram). The mats should be three feet from any wall.

Divide the participants into two teams and instruct one team to take the field while the other team bats. Place the ball on the floor halfway between first base and home.

Fielding players must remain behind the center line until the ball is kicked, and batters must attempt to kick the ball forward (no bunting allowed).

The first player kicks the ball from the designated spot and begins to run the bases. The runner may stop at any base and stay there as long as she wants. There may be any number of players on a base at any time. Play is dead when the ball is returned to the designated spot by the fielding team. A player is out when:

- The kicked ball is caught before it hits anything. A ball hitting the ceiling or wall is safe.

78

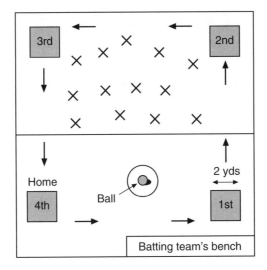

- A runner is touched by the ball, whether thrown or held, while off a base.
- A runner is off the base when the ball is placed back on the designated spot.

Players continue running until all players have batted once. Since runners can keep traveling around the bases if they don't get tagged out, the number of runs a player can score in an inning is limitless.

Runners may run without tagging up at the preceding base when a kicked ball is caught, and the fielding team must still get the ball to the designated spot to stop play.

Variations

- Once teams have been selected, match players of one team to the other. When a player comes to bat, his partner on the fielding team must be the one to put the ball on the designated spot. (This encourages all players to be involved.)
- Designate certain spots as targets (such as the basketball backboard) that, if hit, amount to a home run.

SAFETY

▶ Do not allow sliding into bases.
▶ Keep all bases away from the walls.

NEWCOMBE BALL

Teaching volleyball to young children can be difficult without some adaptations. Here is a game designed to teach the children positioning and team play while they learn the various skills necessary to play volleyball. I always start with this game and then add the skills of serving, bumping, and volleying, adapting the game in each step.

Level

Third grade and up

Skills

Throwing
Passing
Catching
Team building

Equipment

Volleyball net
One gator or utility ball

Description

Divide participants into two teams of 6 to 10 each. Have players on each side of the net form a front and a back row as in volleyball.

Play begins with the player in the back right spot throwing (serving) the ball over the net using any method. The server may move forward as far as needed. Opponents must catch the ball before it hits the floor, make two passes, and throw it back over. Encourage players to let a different person touch the ball each time.

The serving team's goal is to have the ball hit the floor on the other team's side of the net, which scores one point. Only the serving team can score.

Variation

Place blankets over the net so players cannot see their opponents.

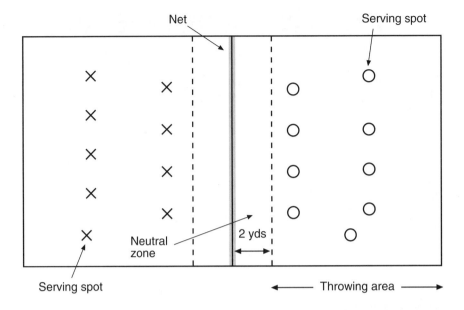

Players are not allowed to walk up to the net and dunk the ball over to the other side. To facilitate this guideline, designate a line across the court that players may not cross.

SIDELINE SOCCER CHAOS

Here is an excellent game to involve all 40-plus participants who show up for intramurals on that rainy day.

Level

Third grade and up

Skills

Kicking
Dribbling (soccer)
Running
Strategy

Equipment

Several gator or soccer balls
Four marked goals
Floor marking tape

Description

If you have many participants, use the entire end walls as goals and tape a goal area on the side walls equal to that distance. You may wish to use benches like in Four Goal Soccer. Continue to mark the goal areas by taping the floor two yards from each wall (see diagram).

Divide participants into four teams and assign each team to one of the walls. Players from each team are given a number. Have each team number off. If there are 10 people on a team, there will be four each of numbers 1 through 10. Place a ball or balls in the center of the floor and call out any two to four numbers. Players with those numbers enter the playing area and try to score on any goal. The other players act as goalies, protecting their goal areas. Players should use proper soccer skills.

On your whistle, the players return to their respective goals; you then call out two to four new numbers, and the game continues. Allow a point for each goal scored.

Goalies may use their hands.

Variation

Try having two games going at once: the end wall teams and the side wall teams play each other and share the ball or balls.

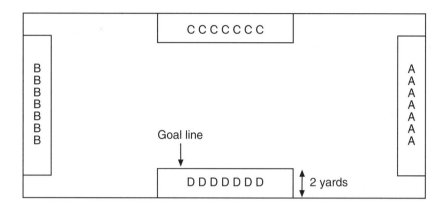

▶ All goals must be scored below waist level.
▶ No body contact is allowed.

ALL-OUT SOCCER

Here is yet another variation on the world's most popular game.

Level

Third grade and up

Skills

Footwork
Running
Strategy
Team building

Equipment

Several gator or soccer balls of two different colors
Two cardboard boxes
Two goal areas (the length of a bench and containing a goal crease)

Description

Divide the participants into two teams and assign each team to a goal. Each team can only score goals with its colored balls and may use one or two goalies to defend its own goal. Shooters cannot enter the other team's goal crease at any time. Set the cardboard boxes along the wall just outside the goal creases. Regular soccer rules apply.

After a goal is scored, the player who scored picks up the ball and places it in the box next to that goal. He then runs to his own goal and removes one of the balls that the other team has scored from that box to put the ball back in play. If there are no balls in the box, the player may take a ball that is not being used from the instructor and put it in the opponent's box.

There should be several balls of both colors in play at all times. Be sure to monitor the balls in play. The winning team is the one with the smaller number of balls in their box when the game ends.

Variation

Use a third colored ball that either team can use, and give it a two- or three-point value.

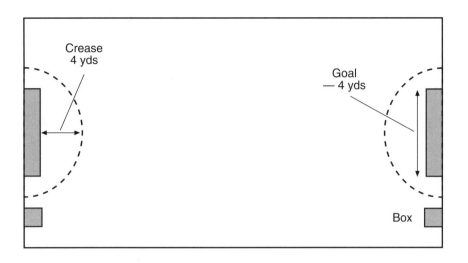

▶ All goals must be scored below waist level.
▶ No body contact is allowed.

PART

ON THE PLAYGROUND

An average elementary school child will spend one to one and a half hours each day on the playground, five days a week, for approximately 40 weeks of the year. That translates into almost 300 hours a year that a child will spend on the school playground during recesses and lunches, and before and during school. What better place to begin the physical development of a child?

Perhaps the best indicator of a need for playground games is the demand CIRA Ontario has had from not just educators, but administrators and parent councils everywhere, for such games. These games get kids active and help reduce the idle time that often leads to the bullying and fighting on playgrounds. As well, I have noted that more often than not these activities serve as an outlet for the energetic and antisocial child.

My present school has five Schlockey games, five tetherball courts, two portable basketball nets, and several hopscotch and four square courts on the outside pavement. Each morning I spend 10 minutes setting out the portable games and ball bin on our play area. On any given recess you can count 50 to 100 children playing, waiting turns, or watching.

Our classroom physical education teachers are in-serviced and encouraged to use their gym classes in the fall and spring to review or introduce the outdoor games to the students. This reinforces the rules by which the school expects the children to play. We always add some of these games into our seasonal play days, and often include them in our intramural program, including Schlockey tournaments and skipping contests.

CHAPTER 10

Fabulous
Four Square

It is never too late to have a good childhood.

FOUR SQUARE (TRADITIONAL)

This game has many variations, depending on the skill level of its participants, and should be adapted accordingly.

Level

Second grade and up

Skills

Catching
Agility
Strategy

Equipment

One utility ball (easily handled by all participants and inflated to allow for good bouncing)
A four square court, six yards square (see diagram)

Description

Four players are needed for a traditional game of four square. Each person is assigned a square, with the goal of the game being to displace the player in square 1. The ball is put in play by the player in square 1, who serves from the back corner of her square by dropping the ball and hitting it with an open hand into one of the other squares. The ball may either not bounce or bounce only once in any square before the player in that square hits the ball into another square.

Misses occur when a player fails to hit the ball into another square or hits it out of bounds. When a miss occurs, the person who is responsible goes to the end of the challenge line and waits to re-enter the game. The other players move up one square, and the first person in the challenge line moves to square 4.

Variations

Variations to the game are endless, depending on the capabilities of the participants. Allow players to juggle or bounce the ball before batting it, or to catch the ball and bounce it before hitting it.

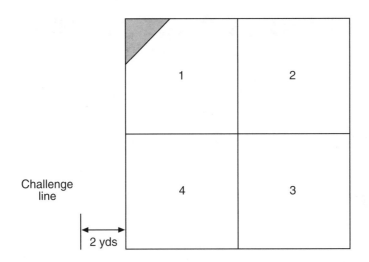

> ► Players in the challenge line should remain back at least two yards.
> ► A traditional four square should be six yards by six yards, with a diagonal line for servers in square 1.

FOUR SQUARE SWITCH

This is the most popular warm-up game that we play on the school pavement.

Level

First grade and up

Skills

Running
Strategy

Equipment

A four square court, six yards square (see diagram)

Description

Four Square Switch is played with one player on each corner and a fifth player, "it", in the middle. The goal of the game is to switch corners without "it" stealing a corner. The person who first gets her foot on the corner has possession of that corner.

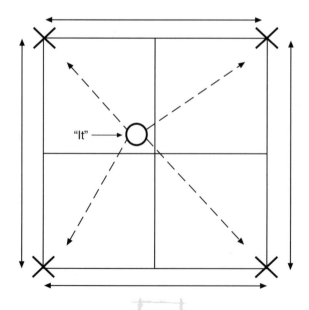

If players are hesitant to switch, "it" places his foot on the center intersection and yells "switch!" and all players must change corners. When "it" steals a corner, the player without a corner becomes "it". If there are subs, then a sub takes over the "it" position.

Four Square Switch can also be played with nine players. Use all eight outside intersections and play in the same manner as the Four Square Switch. You can also use two "its" instead of one.

Remind participants that the person who first gets his foot on the corner is the owner of the corner, and that there is no tagging or use of the hands in this game.

FOUR SQUARE TEAM TAG

This game is similar to Gator Tag (chapter 6), but has fewer participants and a much smaller playing area.

Level

Fourth grade and up

Skills

Catching
Passing
Agility

Equipment

One hand-sized gator or utility ball
A four square court, six yards square (see diagram)

Description

Divide participants into two teams of three or four. Designate one team as the taggers; their goal is to tag the players on the other team while holding the ball. The taggers may not move when they have the ball; they must learn to move without the ball by passing it quickly to a teammate, who can then tag the unsuspecting opponent.

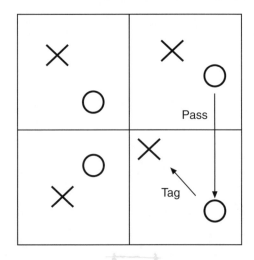

When tagged, a player must leave the court. When all players have been tagged, the teams switch places. As participants become skilled in the game, establish a rule that if the ball is dropped, any one player who has been tagged can re-enter the game.

If you have a 6 yard by 6 yard four square this game works fine, but realize that space is at a premium. The small area helps to speed up the game.

PENNY FOUR SQUARE

This is just another use of the four square court that does not place a premium on skill.

Level

First through fourth grades

Skills

Agility
Ball bouncing

Equipment

A penny (or small pebble)
A utility ball

Description

Place a penny or small pebble on the center of the four square court (see diagram). Players stand outside the court on opposite sides, one player on each side. Players try to knock the penny off the center spot by bouncing the ball back and forth. You can allow the participants to catch the bounce before returning it.

When a player knocks the penny off the center line he scores a point. The penny is replaced and the game continues.

The game can be played to a score of 5 or 10.

Variations

- Add more objects to the center, giving different point values to each object. A player scores the point value of any object knocked off the center line. For example, a penny might be worth 1 point, and a dime worth 5 points.
- Try two players on each team.
- Play the game on a two square (see pages 102-103).

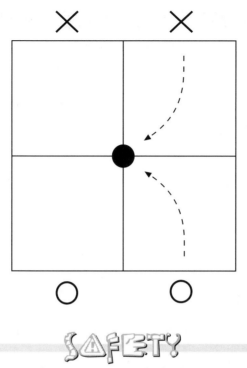

SAFETY

You could play penny four square on half of a four square if space was at a premium, but I wouldn't suggest having two games going on side by side on one four square.

FOUR-PERSON CENTER SQUARE

This version of four square is played in a square with a center square. The center square comes into play on each volley.

Level

Third grade and up

Skills

Catching
Agility

Equipment

A four-person center square (see diagram)

Description

The ball is served by player 1—the ace—to any of the courts. The distinguishing feature of the game is that the ball must always bounce in the center square before entering an opponent's court.

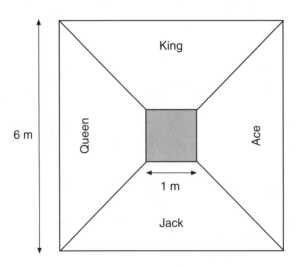

Variation

You can also play this game using a circle with a center circle (see diagram). In all other respects, the game is identical to Four-Person Center Square.

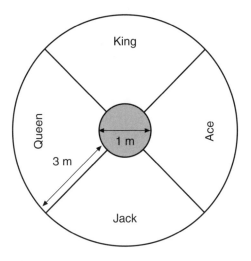

DRIBBLE TAG

Here is an excellent way to practice your basketball dribbling and use your four square court at the same time.

Level

Fourth grade and up

Skills

Dribbling (basketball)
Agility
Strategy

Equipment

A four square court
A basketball

Description

One player dribbles a basketball while trying to tag the other players. The dribbler must be in control of the ball when the tag is made. The player continues until all players have been tagged out. Another

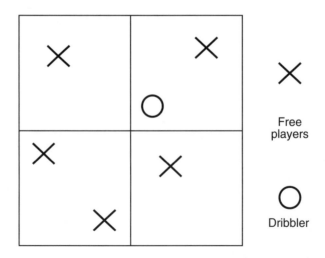

Free players

Dribbler

player is then chosen to be the dribbler. The dribbler tags with the free hand and must control the dribble with the other.

Variations

- When a player is tagged, that player becomes the dribbler.
- When a player is tagged, she becomes frozen, but may be freed if another free player tags her.

TWO SQUARE (TRADITIONAL)

This is a four square game played with only two participants.

Level

Third grade and up

Skills

Catching
Agility
Strategy

Equipment

A two square court (or half of a four square court)
A utility ball

Description

Each player is assigned a square, with the goal to get to and stay in square 1. The ball is put in play when the player in square 1 bounces the ball once and hits it with an open hand into the other player's square. The serve is made from the serving line. The serve must land in the other square, unless the second player chooses to hit it back before it bounces in his square.

Misses occur when a player fails to hit the ball successfully into the other square or hits the ball out of bounds. If the server is at fault, he leaves and the other player takes square 1, and the first person in the challenge line steps into play in the other court. The ousted player goes to the end of the challenge line.

Variations

Endless variations are possible, depending on the skill level of the participants. For example, allow juggling before returning a ball, or even catching if needed.

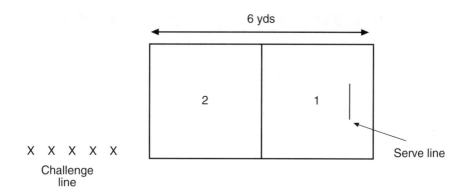

X X X X X

Challenge
line

Strongly suggest that all hits be made with an underhand or push motion. This discourages "dunking."

TWO-PERSON CENTER CIRCLE

This version of four square requires more skill and accuracy from its players.

Level

Fifth grade and up

Skills

Ball skills
Agility
Strategy

Equipment

A two-person center circle, or half of a four-person center circle (see diagram)
A utility ball

Description

The player in court 1 begins by bouncing the ball and hitting it with an open hand into the center circle. The serve is made from the serving line.

The player in court 2 must hit the ball back into the center circle after it is hit there by his opponent, or he may let it bounce one time. The ball must always bounce into the center circle before entering the opponent's court.

If the player in court 1 makes the error, he goes to the end of the challenge line (see diagram). The player in court 2 moves to court 1, and a new player enters court 2 from the challenge line.

Variation

Allow players to juggle or catch the ball before returning it to their opponent.

SAFETY

All balls must be hit with an open hand in an upward motion, like tennis with your hand as the racket.

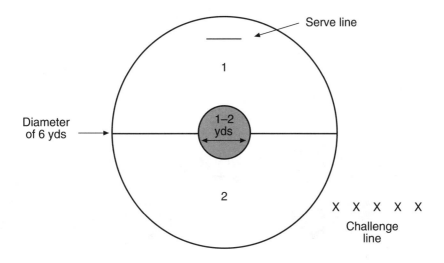

CHAPTER 11

Heaps of Hopscotch

I have learned that my best friend
and I can do anything or nothing
and have the best time.

DRAGON HOPSCOTCH

Dragon Hopscotch has many surprises and is another excellent game for all young students.

Level

Kindergarten through sixth grade

Skill

Agility

Equipment

A hopscotch board drawn on the asphalt (see diagram)
A marker for tossing into squares (such as a pebble)

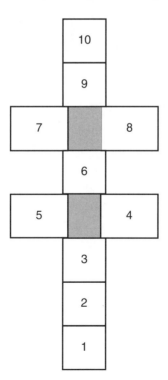

Note: Squares 1, 2, 3, 6, 9, and 10 are 18 inches squared.
Numbers 4, 5, 7, and 8 are 18 inches by 24 inches.

Description

As in other hopscotch games, if a player successfully tosses her marker into the required square, she hops through the course, picking up her marker on the way back. The shaded areas between squares 4 and 5 and 7 and 8 are the "dragons." If any player lands on a dragon, he is sent back to square 2.

Square 6 is also special. If a player is throwing at this square and the marker lands inside the heart, the player may move to square 9. When a player gets to squares 4 and 5, she jumps halfway around once, and again continues to 1. The object is to successfully get to square 10.

ENGLISH HOPSCOTCH

This variation of the traditional game of hopscotch involves a slight but challenging twist.

Level

All ages

Skill

Agility

Equipment

A hopscotch board drawn on the asphalt (see diagram)
A small object to toss into the squares (such as a pebble)

Description

The objective of English Hopscotch is to hop from one square to another, kicking the marker from square to square. The first player tosses his marker into square 1, then hops into the square, kicks the stone out past the baseline with the foot he is hopping on, and then hops out. He then tosses the marker into square 2 and follows the same procedure, moving all the way to square 10.

The player loses his turn as in regular rules of hopscotch, with one addition: if the player fails to kick the marker all the way out over the baseline, he also loses his turn. When one player misses, another takes a turn. On their next turn, players begin on the square they missed in their previous turn. The winner is the player who first completes the 10 squares.

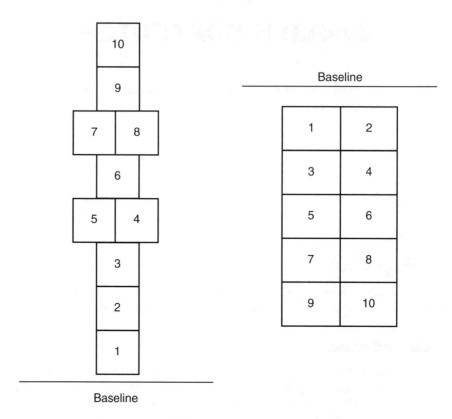

Note: All squares are 18 inches squared.

110

FINNISH HOPSCOTCH

This game is best played with two or three participants.

Level

All ages

Skill

Agility

Equipment

A hopscotch board drawn on the asphalt (see English Hopscotch diagram)
A marker to toss into the squares (such as a pebble)

Description

The challenge of the game is to successfully move through the court in both directions. Each player places a marker in the first square. The first player hops into each single square, and straddles each of the two parallel squares. Upon reaching the end of the court, the player turns around and hops back to the last free square before reaching her own marker. At this point, the player stands on one foot, reaches forward, and picks up her marker without touching a line or any other marker. The player then hops over the square(s) that contain the other markers, and moves out of the court.

If the player makes a mistake, she leaves her marker where it is and waits until the other players have had their turn before taking another turn. If successful upon completing her turn, the same player tosses her marker into the next square. If the marker reaches the correct square and does not fall on a line, the player continues. If not, the marker is placed back into its previous square and the player gives up her turn. This happens throughout the game whenever a player makes an error.

When a player successfully gets back to the first square, she picks up her marker, places it on the back of one hand, and attempts to hop through all the squares and back without dropping the marker, stepping on a line, or stepping in another player's square. If successful, the game is over.

HEAVEN AND EARTH

This hopscotch variation originated in Italy.

Level

All ages

Skill

Agility

Equipment

A hopscotch board drawn on the asphalt (see diagram)
A marker to toss into the squares (such as a pebble)

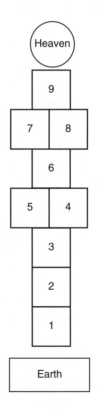

Note: Each square is 18 inches squared.

Description

The object of this hopscotch game is be the first to reach Heaven. Two or three participants may play this game.

Draw a hopscotch board with nine squares and number them from 1 to 9. At the bottom of the first square, draw a rectangle—this is Earth. Draw a circle above the ninth square—this is Heaven. The first player stands on Earth and throws his marker into square 1. If successful, the player hops on one foot into the square, picks up the marker, and hops back to Earth. This is repeated for each square, with the player always returning to Earth. If the player misses, he picks up his marker and lets the next person take her turn. When his turn comes again he continues to throw for the target he last missed.

The first player to successfully reach number 9 and return is declared the winner.

LADDER

This simple hopscotch variation seems to be one of the favorites of my students.

Level

All ages

Skill

Agility

Equipment

A hopscotch board drawn on the asphalt (see diagram)

Description

Paint a large rectangle on the asphalt and divide it into twelve long sections. Instruct players to line up at one end of the "ladder." Standing on one foot, the first player hops to the end square and back. Players may not use two feet and must not touch any lines. They are to imagine that the lines are rotten, crumbling rungs on a ladder. After the first player completes the ladder sections successfully, the second player goes, then the third, and so on.

Note: Each rectangle is 24 inches long and 16 inches wide.

Once the whole line has had a turn, the game becomes more challenging. Players climb the ladder again, but this time they must skip every other square. The next time they must skip two squares, then three, and so on, until eventually the distance between squares is too wide to jump. The person who skips the most squares is declared the winner.

PICKUP HOP/COTCH

This is a good game for the younger, first-time hopscotchers.

Level

All ages

Skill

Agility

Equipment

A hopscotch board drawn on the asphalt (see diagram)
A marker to toss into the squares (such as a pebble)

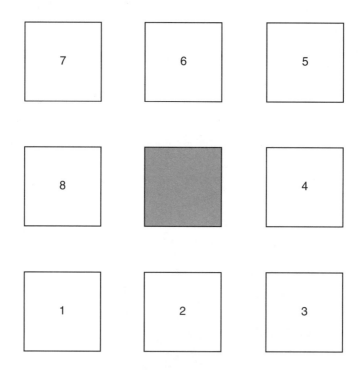

Note: All squares are 18 inches squared. All distances between squares are 6 inches.

Description

The game begins with the first player tossing her marker into the center square and then hopping into square 1, picking up the marker, and hopping out. The player then tosses the marker into the center again, hops into square 1, then into square 2. She then picks up the stone and hops out via square 1. The player continues advancing from square to square, always tossing to the center. The game ends when one player advances through all the numbers successfully.

When a player misses her intended target she picks up her marker and awaits her next turn by again trying for the same number.

PLAYGROUND CALCULATION

Would you like to mix some math skills into your physical education classes? Try this hopscotch game.

Level

All ages

Skills

Agility
Math problem solving

Equipment

A playground "calculator" drawn on the asphalt (see diagram)

1	2	3	+	x
4	5	6	0	÷
7	8	9	–	+
On		Off		Out
Playground computer				

Note: The top 15 squares should be 16 inches squared. On and Off buttons 40 inches by 16 inches.

Description

Draw a diagram of a calculator on a playground blacktop surface. The squares should be big enough for a student's foot to fit in easily. The object of the game is for the first player to hop a specified sequence.

1. Jump on the "on" square.
2. From the "on" square jump to the 5 square.
3. Then jump to the + square.
4. Jump to the 8 square.
5. Jump to the = square.
6. The second player then has to figure out the answer and jump to it. Since the answer of 5 + 8 = 13, the student jumps to the 1 and the 3 squares.
7. After jumping to the number 13, the player jumps to the "off" square.
8. If correct, the second player hops out an equation and the first player must solve it. If there are more than two players, simply continue down the list. If a player hops the wrong answer or steps on a line, she loses a point. All players start with five points.

SWAMP HOPSCOTCH

Like Pickup Hopscotch, there is no equipment required for this game, and it helps the younger players with their numbers.

Level

All ages

Skill

Agility

Equipment

A hopscotch board drawn on the asphalt (see diagram)

12	13	14	1
11			2
10			3
9			4
8	7	6	5

Note: Each square is 18 inches squared.

Description

Instruct the players to imagine themselves in a wet, hot, humid swamp. The hopscotch squares are patches of dry land and the lines are swampy waters, infested with bullfrogs, leeches, and maybe even a crocodile or two.

The object of the game is to maneuver through the swamp. Starting in square 1, each player must hop on one foot to square 14. Once he reaches the last square, he hops back to square 1. Do not be fooled—once the first square is reached, the game is not over. Players have to hop to square 14 and back again, except this time they can only hop on the odd numbers. The third time, they hop on only the even numbers. The fourth time, they hop the sequence 1, 4, 7, 10, 14, and back.

Remind players never to step on a line or in the middle of the playing area, or else they might be lunch for a hungry crocodile.

ALPHABET HOPSCOTCH

This is a great game for teaching children how to spell.

Level

All ages

Skill

Agility

Equipment

An alphabet hopscotch drawn on asphalt (see diagram)

Description

The objective of Alphabet Hopscotch is to jump from A to B, B to C, and so on, without touching the lines. Vary the game by spelling names, places, and things. Blank squares can be used as free jump spaces.

G	F	U		V	K
O	Y	N	S		L
		I	Q	E	
T		Z		R	X
D	W	M	C	B	
P	J		A	H	

Note: Each square is 16 inches squared.

NUMBER HOPSCOTCH

Play hopscotch and learn your numbers at the same time. After all, mathematics should be fun, too!

Level

All ages

Skill

Agility

Equipment

A hopscotch board drawn on the asphalt (see diagram)

Description

- Jump numbers progressively upward.
- Jump numbers progressively backward.
- Ask opponent to hop an equation—for example, $3 \times 4 = 12$.
- Blank squares can be used as free jump spaces.

29	4	13	28	19	6
24		5	25		27
3	14	18	8	31	7
30	21	2	32	20	17
23		10	26		9
1	11	15	22	12	16

Note: Each square is 16 inches squared.

CHAPTER 12

Fancy Footwork

You can discover more about a person in an
hour of play than in a year of conversation.

–Plato

JUMP THE SHOT

Skipping can come in many disguises. Here is still another way to use a rope, and up to 12 players.

Level

First grade and up

Skill

Agility

Equipment

One long jump rope
One beanbag

Description

This game is played with 4 to 12 participants. Take a long rope and attach a small beanbag to one end. The players form a circle, and one person goes to the center. The center player holds the rope by the free end and swings the rope along the ground around the circle. All the players must jump over the rope. Anyone who steps on the rope becomes the center player. To make the game more difficult, increase the turning speed of the rope, change the direction, or add a second turner, back to back with the first. Some communication between the turners is needed.

The turners may sing this song if they wish:

Whirly bird, whirly bird
Jump so high
Whirly bird, whirly bird
Can you fly?

SAFETY

Be sure the turner keeps the rope at ground level. If the turner spins too fast, she could get dizzy, so change direction, or change turners frequently.

ALL TOGETHER

This simple skipping game emphasizes group cooperation.

Level

All ages

Skills

Footwork
Agility
Team building

Equipment

A single or double-dutch jump rope
Laminated cue cards (with words for the chants)

Description

This long jump rope game can be done with four to eight participants. Select two rope turners and begin. All players begin to chant the *All Together* verse (see below) as the turners begin a steady turn of the rope. Players enter, one at a time, as they hear their birthday month called. If there are more than one for any month, the chant stops or repeats until all players from that month have had a turn to get in. Then the chant continues until all months have been called. Once all players are in, they exit as the day of the month of their birthday is called. Players who miss become the turner.

> All in together boys
> This fine weather girls
> When is your birthday?
> Please jump in
> January, February, March,
> April, May, June, July,
> August, September, October,
> November, December
> All in together boys
> This fine weather girls

When is your birthday?
Please jump out
1, 2, 3 . . . 31

In long rope skipping, a large group can skip together on this chant.

Variations

Add these other chants for your long rope games:

Ice Cream Soda

Ice cream soda
Lemonade hearts
Tell me the names
Of your sweethearts
A, B, C, D . . .

With the turners using a long rope, a new jumper may run through on each letter. If using a short rope and only one jumper, turners can turn the rope more quickly on each letter.

Happy Birthday

All in together
This fine weather
January, February, March . . .

The jumper runs in on the month of his or her birthday.

All out together
This fine weather
January, February, March . . .

The jumper runs out on the month of his or her birthday.

I'm an Athlete

This skipping chant is guaranteed to get the heart racing! Select two players to turn the rope while the other players form a line and take turns jumping in and singing the following song:

I'm an athlete
Dressed in blue
Here are the things
That I can do

Stand at attention
Stand at ease
Bend my elbows
Bend my knees
Salute to the captain
Bow to the queen
Turn my back on the
Yellow submarine
I can do the heel-toe
I can do the splits
I can do the wiggle-woggle
Just like this

Players can then create their own zany original actions—for example, a wiggle-woggle can be anything the skipper wants.

Apples, Peaches, Pears, and Plums

This is a cooperative skipping game in which every player uses his or her best skipping skills. Two players are chosen to turn the rope, and the others form a line. All of the players sing the following verse.

Apples, peaches
Pears and plums
Tell me when
Your birthday comes,
January, February . . .

When the player's birthday month is called out, he or she jumps in to skip. Eventually, when all the players are jumping, the days of the month are called out: 1, 2, 3 . . . 31. When a player's birthday is called out, he or she must jump out. If any player stops the rope, he or she takes the place of one of the rope turners, who then becomes a skipper.

As in all skipping games, a pattern of turning should be taught that is at the level of the participants.

ABC

This skipping game tests the participants' knowledge of the alphabet and is played with four or more skippers.

Level

All ages

Skill

Agility

Equipment

A single or double-dutch jump rope

Description

Have all the players form a line, and select two players to turn the rope. The first player jumps in, calls out "A," jumps out, and runs around to the end of the line. The next player repeats the pattern, except he calls out "B," and so on. Any player who interrupts the rhythm in any way becomes a rope turner. The player who has "Z" stops the game by catching the rope between her feet.

Variation

Have the participants recite the alphabet in other languages.

Teach all students the proper turning technique, emphasizing a steady speed and good height on each turn.

EL RELOJ

This Guatemalan skipping game involves large numbers, counting, and some cooperation to work properly.

Level

Third grade and up

Skills

Footwork
Agility
Team building

Equipment

One long jump rope
Bean bag

Description

Twelve players stand in a circle, representing the numbers on a clock. The thirteenth player stands in the middle of the circle. The group counts to 12, then the turner begins to turn the rope. On each turn the turner speeds up slightly. The players must jump over the rope each time it passes by. See Jump the Shot diagram on p. 126.

When players touch or stop the rope, they are eliminated. The game continues until only one person is left. As the game winds down the turner may raise the level of the rope to make it harder for the jumpers.

Variation

Have two turners back to back, each with a rope, turning at the same speed.

Be sure to demonstrate this game and instruct children on the skills needed for it before letting them play.

CARIBOU SKIPPING

This skipping activity is an adaptation of the Inuit or Eskimo version, in which a caribou skin is wrapped around the rope.

Level

Fourth grade and up

Skills

Footwork
Agility

Equipment

A double-dutch rope
A potato sack
Duct tape

Description

Using a long jump rope with a potato sack (representing a caribou skin) wrapped around the middle and taped securely, two individuals swing the rope (see figure). One competitor stands in the middle facing the sack. The rope is swung back and forth without going over the skipper's head. After three swings, the rope goes over her head. The process is repeated: *1, 2, 3, over; 1, 2, 3, over.*

Each time the player jumps, she must quickly adjust herself in order to be facing the sack before it comes back. Be careful—when the potato sack goes over her head, the participant does not have to turn around. When the rope simply goes back and forth, the jumper must turn around each time since the rope is now behind her, and she must always be facing the sack. But when it goes under her and continues overhead, it comes down in front of the jumper, and she shouldn't turn around.

As competitors become more efficient, the turners begin to move more quickly.

SAFETY

▶ Turners need to use both hands, as the rope is heavier with the bag attached.

▶ Both turners and skippers need to know the *1, 2, 3, over* cadence before beginning.

▶ Turners should begin slowly and make sure the sack touches the floor on each pass and clearly goes over the skipper's head on the over swing.

CHINESE SKIPPING

Every time I do this one at a workshop, one or two teachers tell me, "Oh, I remember doing this one." They then proceed to get up and teach us a new routine.

Level

All ages

Skills

Footwork
Agility

Equipment

Rubber bands

Description

Loop rubber bands together, then tie ends to make a loop about 8-10 feet in diameter (see figure).

Place rubber bands around the ankles of two participants, who stand about three yards apart with their feet shoulder-width apart. The third person jumps a pattern, such as *Mississippi* or *British Isles* (see diagram).

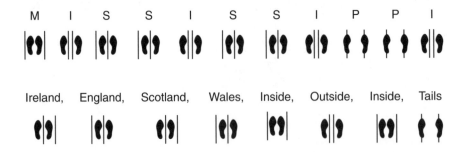

If he completes the pattern without making a mistake, the two end people move the rubber band rope up to their shins. The third person repeats the pattern with the rubber bands at the shins, then at the knees. He continues until he makes a mistake; then he takes an end of the rubber band loop and lets someone else jump.

SAFETY

Always start the rubber band loop at a low level in order that the first few turns are easy for each participant.

CHAPTER 13

Off the Wall

If life gives you a lemon, make lemonade.

ARE YOU COMING OUT, SIR?

When I first tried this with my third-grade gym class, they not only mastered it in 20 minutes but came up with several new actions of their own.

Level

Third grade and up

Skill

Agility

Equipment

One rubber or tennis ball per participant
One old pair of pantyhose or socks per participant
Laminated chart with words to the chant, posted on a near wall

Description

Push a ball into the bottom of a long wool sock or one leg of a pair of panty hose, tying it securely in a half (overhand) knot.

Participants stand with their backs against a wall and swing the stocking, bouncing the ball from side to side off the wall while chanting a verse (see below). Each time they say the word *Sir* in the chant, participants bounce the ball off the wall. Players can create their own patterns, including bouncing the ball under their left leg, under their arms, overhead, and between their legs.

Start with the stocking in the right hand and try to speed up the chant each time. Students should perform the actions in the proper order. The actions and sequence always remain the same, unless the participants wish to make their own changes.

Each child has his or her own piece of equipment. First, allow for experimentation. Second, teach the three basic actions (R = bounce ball against the wall to your right; L = bounce ball against the wall to your left; LL = bounce ball under your left leg as you lift it). Third, teach the chant.

Hello, hello, hello, *Sir*
  R   L   R   LL

No, *Sir.* Why, *Sir?*
R-LL   R-LL

Where'd you get the cold, *Sir?*
  R   L R   LL

What were you doing there, *Sir?*
  R   L   R LL

How many did you catch, *Sir?*
  R   L   R LL

That's enough for me, *Sir*
  R   L   R LL

Are you coming out, *Sir?*
  R   L   R LL

Because I've got a cold, *Sir*
  R   L   R   LL

At the North Pole, *Sir*
  R   L   R LL

Catching polar bears, *Sir.*
  R   L   R LL

One, *Sir,* two, *Sir,* three, *Sir*
R - LL R - LL R - LL

Allow ample room between participants.

DONKEY

From the time the snow melts until school is dismissed in June, this game always takes up part of a wall somewhere at my school.

Level

Fourth grade and up

Skills

Catching
Throwing

Equipment

One tennis ball
Gloves (optional)

Description

This game can be played with two to eight players. The players scatter themselves out several yards from the wall. The player with the ball throws it off the wall, and any player may catch it in the air or after it has bounced on the ground. If it is caught cleanly, then the player catching it throws it back to the wall and the game repeats itself. If the ball is dropped, then the player who drops it must run to touch the wall before any other player retrieves the ball and throws it to the wall. If the ball hits the wall before the player gets there, then that player gets a *d*. Once a player has spelled *donkey,* he's out of the game.

Variation

Spell a shorter word (such as *pig).*

▶ Use only tennis balls, since they are soft and bounce well.
▶ Use a well spaced area.

ONE HUNDRED

This game is similar to Donkey, but has a different system for scoring.

Level

Fourth grade and up

Skills

Catching
Throwing

Equipment

One tennis ball
Gloves (optional)
Chalk

Description

With the chalk, draw a line parallel to the wall, 5 yards from the wall (see diagram). This game is best played with five or more participants. The thrower tosses the ball off the wall so it lands beyond the five-yard line. Players get 10 points for catching the ball, and lose 10 points if they drop the ball. They get 5 points for a first-bounce catch and 3 points for cleanly picking the ball up after the second bounce. The same number of points are lost if the ball is dropped. If the ball is dropped, play is stopped immediately. The ball is returned to the thrower and the game is repeated until someone reaches 100. That person then becomes the thrower. The game can also be played to 50.

Participants should be able to play in an area that is no more than 10 yards wide.

Variations

- Score points only for balls caught before the ball bounces.
- A ball that touches the ground is a dead ball.

Use only a tennis ball, as it bounces well and is not hard.

SEVEN-UP

Seven-Up combines the skills of throwing and catching with a variety of individual moves, and is a good game to play even if you are alone.

Level

Third grade and up

Skills

Throwing
Catching
Agility

Equipment

One small rubber or tennis ball

Description

Players should stand approximately five yards from the wall. Each player takes a turn performing the Seven-Up actions against a wall. If a player is successful, she waits for her turn to come around again; if she makes a mistake, she is eliminated.

Vary the game by changing the actions. Different movements that may be incorporated include clapping and using one hand.

7-up	Throw the ball against the wall, catch it
6-up	Throw, bounce, catch
5-up	Bounce on ground, against wall, catch
4-up	Bounce under right leg, against wall, catch
3-up	Bounce under left leg, against wall, catch
2-up	Bounce under spread legs, against wall, catch
1-up	Drop the ball on a bounce, turn around in a circle, and catch it before it bounces a second time

CHAPTER 14

Outdoor Games With a Twist

People rarely succeed at anything
unless they have fun doing it.

TWO-FOOT SHUFFLE

This idea came from Tim Rafter, a teacher in Winnipeg, during a break at a CIRA executive meeting in British Columbia. If you are looking for a new way to choose between two people or for a quick, fun activity, try this game.

Level

All ages

Skill

Agility

Equipment

None

Description

This game is played in pairs. One player is the leader while the other player is the opponent. The two players face each other, standing only a foot and a half apart, with feet shoulder-width apart (see diagram).

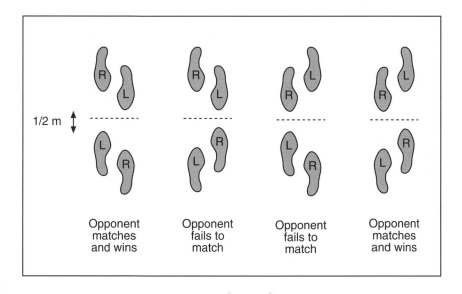

| Opponent matches and wins | Opponent fails to match | Opponent fails to match | Opponent matches and wins |

The leader and the first opponent jump and high-five each other and land with their feet still shoulder-width apart. As soon as the players' feet make contact with the ground, they immediately shuffle or switch their feet into one of two positions. If the opponent does not have the same foot forward as the leader, then the leader gets a point. If the opponent does have the same foot forward as the leader, the opponent takes the leader role. The game is played to five points.

SCHLOCKEY

Schlockey is a fast-paced, action-packed, exciting game played with bladeless "Schlockey sticks". I have promoted this game across Canada, and I even gave it the name "Schlockey," which is *school* and *hockey* combined.

Level

Second grade and up

Skill

Agility

Equipment

A Schlockey game box (see figure)
Two Schlockey sticks (old hockey sticks with the blades cut off and the ends taped)
One hockey puck

Supplies

28 feet of 2" x 6" pressure-treated wood

> 2 lengths of 8 feet
> 3 lengths of 4 feet

One 4' x 8' x 3/4" pressure-treated plywood
Lots of 3" spiral, galvanized nails or screws
Paint

Description

The game is played on a 4' by 8' arena. The arena has 6" high side boards, end boards, and a center line or board that contains two puck ports, the openings. Only participating players are allowed in the playing area, with spectators and waiting players remaining in the viewing area.

Each player selects a side and a direction in which to shoot. Players may wish to use a forehand for a better shot at the opponent's end hole. In some cases, a player will be forced to use a backhand grip. The puck is placed on the top of the center board.

The players then touch sticks three times, saying *N-H-L* or *1-2-3*. At the third tap, players go for the puck, which will fall into one side. The players then shuffle back and forth, trying to shoot the puck through the opponent's end hole. Players can put only "schticks" (Schlockey sticks) on the surface. No body parts are allowed in the Schlockey box.

 SUCCESS STORY

There are always 50 students lined up to play each recess at the five games at my school. This is a great activity for developing the arms. CIRA Ontario has a Schlockey booklet that thoroughly describes how to make and play Schlockey.

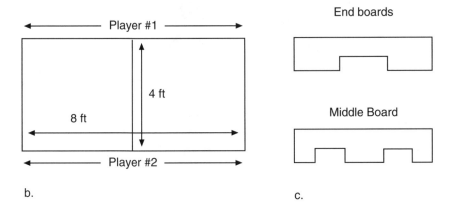

Note: cutouts 3" high by 4" wide.

SAFETY

▶ Paint a safety zone around each game and a waiting zone for players next in line.
▶ Teach the game to all participants before playing.
▶ Do not allow high sticks, swinging of sticks, or any other abuse of the equipment.
▶ Players may play only one game and then switch with other players. The only exception is when there is no one waiting in line.
▶ Do not allow jamming of sticks into the holes or blocking of a hole with a stick.

DICE ROLL

This is an excellent counting game played in class, during gym, or at recess under a tree.

Level

Children who can read dice and count to 100

Skill

Math problem solving

Equipment

Five dice

Description

Each player takes a turn rolling the five dice and accumulating points according to the format below until a predetermined score is obtained (such as 10, 20, 50, or 100 points).

1 pair	1 point
2 pairs	5 points
Triplets	10 points
Triplets and a pair	15 points
4 of a kind	15 points
5 of a kind	20 points
A straight (1, 2, 3, 4, 5)	20 points

TETHERBALL

Tetherball should be played with many variations and rules. I will describe one, but the participants will often have to play a while before finding a set of rules that is suitable.

Level

Third grade and up

Skills

Agility
Footwork
Strategy
Hand–eye coordination

Equipment

A tetherball stand

Description

Tetherball can be played with two to four players. The server starts the game by striking the held ball with his hand or fist in the direction of choice.

As the ball travels around the pole, the server tries to strike it again and again in the direction of the original serve in an attempt to wind the ball completely around the pole. The opponents try to wind the rope around the pole by hitting the ball in the opposite direction. All players must stay in their half of the tetherball court (see diagram). The players who first wind the ball around the pole completely in their direction are the winners.

Variation

Allow catching of the ball before striking.

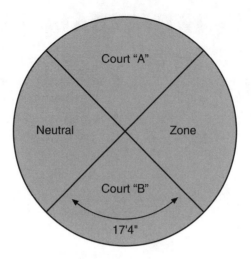

Court "A"

Neutral   Zone

Court "B"

17'4"

This game requires teacher supervision and teaching prior to participants playing on their own.

ROCKIN' ROBIN

Singing games are almost forgotten as playground games, but teachers who supervise playgrounds will tell you that sometime during each year they will hear them. Who has taught these children? Where did they hear these songs? They are passed down somehow from generation to generation and they *do* survive.

Level

All ages

Skill

Agility

Equipment

Perhaps a laminated copy of the song. As before, some of these activities work best with a song or chant. Participants often do not know these songs or chants, and need a visual aid to help them get started. This saves the time that would be needed to teach the song or chant by rote.

Description

Participants stand in a circle of four. They sing the song and follow the actions.

Song	Actions
Tweet, tweet, tweet	(Hold hands on each side and swing arms)
And away we go	
Go rocking in the treetop	(Rocking motion, clap own hands for four beats)
All day long	
Huffing and a-puffing	(Slap both hands with partner to your left four times)
And a-singing this song	
All the little birdies	(Repeat with partner on the right)
On Jaybird Street	

Love to hear the robin

(Clap one hand left partner and one hand right partner four times)

Go tweet, tweet, tweet

Rockin' robin—tweet, tweet, tweet

(Clap own hands twice and slap hands with partner across from you)

Rockin' robin—tweet, tweet, tweet

Repeat

Go rockin' robin, we're really

(Clap own hands once, left to left of partner across, clap own hands once, right to right to partner across from you)

Gonna rock tonight

MARBLE SHOOT

Marbles have long been a playground favorite. The many variations always provide a great opportunity to work on hand-eye coordination, concentration, and competition.

Level

Most children from kindergarten to grade 3 can pick up this skill.

Skill

Hand–eye coordination

Equipment

Marbles
Chalk

Description

Children initially need to be taught how to properly shoot a marble. Place the thumb just behind the first finger's nail and place the marble in the spot where the thumb nail touches the first finger. The remaining fingers can be closed or open, depending on the player. Happy shooting!

This game may be played with any number of participants, each with the same number of similar marbles. Mark a starting line on the ground. The first player shoots a marble from the starting line onto the playing area. The second player tries to hit the first player's marble with her shot. If she does, she keeps both marbles, and the next player in line shoots to begin again. If the second player misses, then the third player attempts to hit either marble to collect both marbles.

This pattern continues until only one player has marbles or players run out of time.

Variation

Create a *castle* for each player consisting of four marbles. Three of the marbles are arranged in a triangle, with the fourth perched on the top. All triangles should be an equal distance from the shooting line and close enough to be hittable (one yard). Players take turns shooting at the targets to dislodge the marbles. If a player hits a castle and dislodges it, he gets his marble back and gets to keep the castle. If he misses, he picks up his marble and waits his next turn.

PUTTING MARBLES

Here is a marble game that works well on pavement when the field is too wet from rain.

Children initially need to be taught how to properly shoot a marble. Place the thumb just behind the first finger's nail and place the marble in the spot where the thumb nail touches the first finger. The remaining fingers can be closed or open depending on the player. Happy shooting!

Level

All ages

Skill

Hand–eye coordination

Equipment

Marbles
Chalk

Description

Each player needs five marbles. Draw a small circle about 10 inches in diameter on the pavement. This circle is called the "pot." Draw a shooting line about one to two yards from the pot. The players take turns shooting their own marbles toward the pot until all marbles have been shot.

The player ending up closest to the pot gets to "putt" first for the pot with his closest marble. Putting is done with a flick of the index finger. As long as his putts result in a marble going into the pot, he continues to putt. He putts only his marbles. If he putts and accidentally knocks in someone else's marble, he loses his turn. When he misses, the next closest person begins, and so on. The player to putt their final marble into the pot first wins all the marbles.

Variation

The first player to putt successfully wins all the marbles.

RING GAME

The object of many marble games is to earn your opponent's marbles. Here's one where a player can earn many new "shooters" to add to her collection.

Level

All ages

Skill

Hand–eye coordination

Equipment

Marbles
Chalk

Description

Children initially need to be taught how to properly shoot a marble. Place the thumb just behind the first finger's nail and place the marble in the spot where the thumb nail touches the first finger. The remaining fingers can be closed or open depending on the player. Happy shooting!

This game begins with each player contributing an equal number of marbles to make up a circle of 16 or more, with space between the marbles. Draw a shooting line at a distance each player can ably shoot from.

A larger marble is placed in the center of the circle. Players take turns shooting to hit the center marble. Any marbles that miss are left on the playing area. When the center marble is hit, the shooter gets to collect the 16 marbles and any that were shot and missed.

Variation

Each player puts a large marble into the center and the winner gets all 16 marbles, all missed shots, and all large marbles.

BOUNCE EYE

Here is one marble game in which you don't need to be a great shooter to be successful.

Level

All ages

Skill

Agility

Equipment

Marbles
Chalk

Description

Two or more players are needed, each with an equal number of marbles. Draw a circle approximately one yard in diameter on the pavement.

Each player places two marbles side by side in the center of the circle. Players stand outside the circle and take turns dropping marbles from head high and arm's length away. Players get to keep any marbles they knock out of the circle, along with their own marble, and continue their turn. If they miss, their marble stays in the circle.

The game ends when no marbles remain in the circle.

Variation

If a player simply hits a marble when she drops hers, then she gets that marble, her own, and another turn.

CIRA ONTARIO

Mission

CIRA's mission is to encourage, promote, and develop active living, healthy lifestyle, and personal growth through intramural and recreational programs within the educational community.

Your Professional Association

CIRA Ontario is one of ten provincial Intramural and Recreation Associations under the CIRA umbrella. Located in Ottawa, the National Office provides a variety of programs and services to its provincial members. In conjunction with CIRA Ontario's Executive Committee and Office Staff, the provincial and national organizations work hand in hand to promote active living and active schools.

CIRA and CIRA Ontario Member Benefits

- The CIRA Publications Catalogue containing over 160 practical resources
- 8 Bulletins per year packed with new games, ideas, and news including the Leader featuring leadership information, tips, and stories
- 4 INPUT Newsletters from CIRA ONTARIO published quarterly
- Special Program Materials, such as Choices and Decisions: Taking Charge of Your Life, Recess Revival
- Ready-to-use Resources for all educational levels - Elementary, Secondary, Post Secondary
- Special member prices for CIRA and CIRA Ontario resources
- Student Leadership Development Program Materials
- Provincial and National conferences and workshops

Take advantage of CIRA 's knowledge and exper tise by joining today!

For more information, contact CIRA Ontario, c/o Mohawk College, P.O. Box 2034, Hamilton, Ontario, L8N 3T2, CANADA. Tel: (905) 575-2083; Fax: (905) 575-2264; E-mail: harknem@mail.mohawkc.on.ca.

	Member	Student	Life
One year	$45	$25	$400
Two years	$85	$45	

ABOUT THE AUTHORS

Pat Doyle is the president of the Canadian Intramural Recreation Association of Ontario (CIRA Ontario), an organization that encourages, promotes, and develops active living, healthy lifestyles, and personal growth through intramural and recreation programs within the educational community. He has written seven resources for CIRA Ontario, including *Great Gator Games, Mass Appeal,* and *Awesome Asphalt Activities.* He has also conducted workshops across Canada.

Doyle has more than 26 years of experience as a physical education teacher at the kindergarten through sixth grade levels. He lives in Kitchener, Ontario, with his wife Francine and their children. In his spare time he enjoys cooking, reading, and jogging; he has completed 11 marathons.

The past president of CIRA Ontario, **Michelle Harkness** currently serves as the executive assistant for CIRA Ontario and as manager of student life and reservations at Mohawk College. She is a recreation and leisure studies graduate with 25 years of experience in recreation programming.

Harkness and her husband Glenn live in Hamilton, Ontario. In her free time she enjoys traveling, participating in the school council, and doing volunteer work.